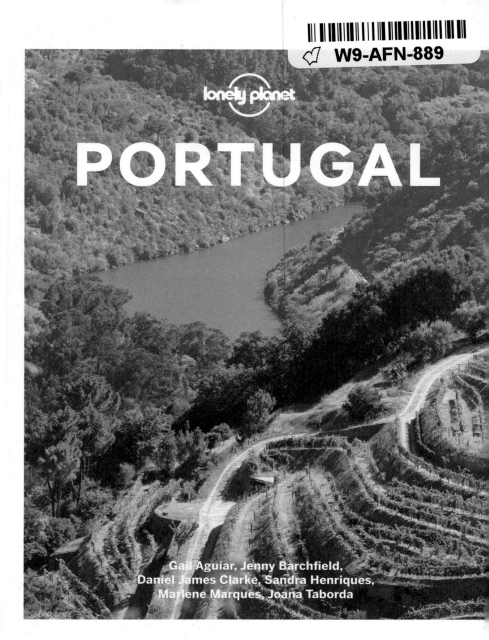

lonely planet

PORTUGAL

Gail Aguiar, Jenny Barchfield,
Daniel James Clarke, Sandra Henriques,
Marlene Marques, Joana Taborda

Contents

MARCIN KRZYZAK/SHUTTERSTOCK ©

Above Bica funicular, Lisbon

FOODIE FACTS

Portugal's cuisine is Mediterranean-based, but largely influenced by its colonial past.

Bread and wine are a regular presence at every table.

Although the food is meat- and fish-heavy, vegan and vegetarian dishes do exist.

MED CUISINE
WITH SPICE

▬▬ Portugal's cultural melting pot comes through most genuinely in food. Whether you're tasting the latest creations of a Michelin-starred chef or dipping a chunk of bread in a homemade-style *bacalhau à lagareiro* (salted cod baked in olive oil), that flavour in your taste buds transcends centuries and boundaries. Dinners are always a sit-down, lingering experience that doesn't end until the last drop of your post-meal espresso.

PORTION SIZES

At *tascas* and other typical eateries, single portions are often large enough to feed two. Order a *meia dose* (half portion) if you don't have much of an appetite.

Left Grilled sardines **Right** Selection of *petiscos* (small plates) **Below** Traditional Portuguese starters

CHEF TIPS

At traditional (often family-owned) restaurants, embrace the tips of the resident chef: often a mother, aunt or grandmother.

↑ PETISCOS

In some restaurants, a spread of *petiscos* (starters) is brought to your table, no questions asked. Before you start to nibble, note that they're *not* complimentary.

▶ Learn more about *petiscos* on p172

Best Food Experiences

▶ Dip your toes in the local foodie scene, exploring Lisbon's traditional and contemporary restaurants (p52)

▶ Explore (and taste) the cultural background of a pork-free sausage in Mirandela (p225)

▶ Feast on fresh fish in the Algarve (p144)

▶ Indulge in hearty Alentejo cuisine; wine pairing optional (p131)

PORTUGAL BEST EXPERIENCES

FAMILY
FUN

The close-to-300 days of sunshine is a great excuse to spend time outdoors, letting the kids blow off steam while exploring local biodiversity. Historic and prehistoric sites make for great opportunities for fun learning. And the three days of Carnaval, celebrated all over the country in February/March, are perfect for children and adults alike to dress up as their favourite fictional characters.

FAMILY PRICES

Some attractions offer special family prices. Family is used as a broad term for two adults and two children, or one adult and one child.

Left Carnaval parade, Loulé
Right Palácio Nacional da Pena, Sintra **Below** FIESA Sand City

MUSEUM ACTIVITIES

Most activities for children at museums are held in Portuguese. If one of them catches your eye, ask beforehand if they speak your language.

CHILDREN'S FILMS

International films for kids under six are released in two versions: subtitled (VO – *versão original*) and dubbed (VP – *versão Portuguesa*).

Best Family Experiences

▶ Explore medieval castles and luxurious palaces in the Unesco World Heritage town of Sintra (p84)

▶ Slide down vertiginous water slides in the sunny Algarve (p160)

▶ Observe and take part in an ancient pagan ritual in Podence (p221)

▶ Discover the pop-culture sand sculptures at FIESA Sand City (p161)

▶ Find Nemo and study starfish at Sea Life Porto (p193)

IN TOUCH
WITH NATURE

Portugal's mild weather throughout the year and its large number of parks and protected areas allow for weekend family picnics, wildlife observation outings or outdoor group sports. From green refuges amid urban spaces to boat trips to explore ocean caves, the outdoors will welcome you in a myriad of ways.

→ LOCAL GARDENS
Urban parks and gardens often double as venues for unannounced kids' birthday parties and other family reunions.
► For plenty of Porto parks, see p182

Left Snorkelling, Reserva Natural das Berlengas **Right** Jardim do Infante Dom Henrique, Porto **Below** Peneda-Gerês National Park

PARK PICNICS
A lot of Portugal's parks have picnic areas but grills may be removed for safety reasons in the summer during forest fire season.

↑ NATURAL & NATIONAL PARKS
Portugal has 13 natural parks and only one national park (Peneda-Gerês). With a wide variety of habitats, Portugal's protected areas provide excellent opportunities for birdwatching. Given Portugal's long coastline, the country is also well placed for boat trips to view marine life, including dolphins, pelagic fish and even sea turtles.

Best Outdoor Experiences

► Discover tranquillity and tropical trees at the Jardim Botânico de Lisboa (p72)

► Explore where dunes meet scrubland at Parque Natural da Serra da Arrábida (p91)

► Scuba dive at the ocean caves of the Berlengas' islands (p98)

► Observe Iberian wolves in the wild at Parque Natural de Montesinho (p226)

► Challenge your friends to a forest-based paintball match at Parque Aventura (p155)

HIT THE
TRAILS

█████ It doesn't matter if you're just getting started or your weathered boots are covered with the dust of a thousand hikes – in Portugal there is a trail for everyone. Explore the country's only national park, uncover rolling hills and roiling cascades, or feel the salt on your skin as you hike the coast.

Best Hiking Experiences

▶ **Merge with mystical Sintra, hiking in the Parque da Pena** (p85)

▶ **Take it slow and embrace the Alentejo vibe at Serra d'Ossa** (p111)

▶ **Cover Alentejo and the Algarve rambling on the Rota Vicentina** (p143)

▶ **Visit 12 historic villages while tramping the 600km Grand Route** (p163)

TOP NEIFY/GETTY IMAGES ©. BOTTOM: HANS SLEGERS/SHUTTERSTOCK ©

★ RESPONSIBLE HIKING

Particularly in Biosphere Reserves and natural parks or other protected areas, stay on the trails and respect local wildlife.

HUNTING SEASON

Mid-August to late-February is hunting season in Portugal. When hitting the trails, look for the red-and-white signs saying *zona de caça*.

Above left Parque da Pena, Sintra **Left** Hiking the Rota Vicentina

SADDLE UP
& CYCLE

Pedal along the rugged coast or brave the hilly inland and uncover remote villages. Go solo or on a family adventure. Hop on your favourite two-wheel and bike through Portugal any time of the year, exploring at your own pace or booking a guided tour with expert cyclists.

Best Cycling Experiences

▶ Rent a bike and explore riverside Porto, discovering palaces, forts and bridges along the way (p188)

▶ Cycle across the Algarve on the Via Algarviana (p153)

▶ Visit the remote villages of the Northeast on Rota da Terra Fria (p230)

TOP: GUAXINIM/SHUTTERSTOCK ©. BOTTOM: MELISSA GRUNDEMANN/SHUTTERSTOCK ©

ACCOMMODATION

Wild camping is not allowed, so plan your stays between different stages of a route. There are sure to be plenty of accommodation options along the way.

★ RESPONSIBLE CYCLING

Going rogue could have devastating consequences for local wildlife, so stay on the path! Some trails cross private property, with permission of the owners; obey signs and be respectful.

Above left Cyclist, Cabo de São Vicente (p143) **Left** Bike tour, Torre de Belém, Lisbon (p67)

FABULOUS
FESTIVITIES

Pick any month in the calendar, and some place in Portugal is most likely commemorating something. From nationwide celebrations of public holidays to super-niche food and cultural festivals, any excuse is great to party. During the summer, the season picks up speed, with festivals ranging from musical events with top line-ups to small-town fairs and fetes.

→ MUSIC FESTIVALS

Dozens of music festivals crowd the Portuguese events calendar in the summer. Diversity reigns, so pick according to your favourite genre, location or travelling dates.

Left Festival Internacional de Chocolate, Óbidos **Right** Festival F, Faro **Below** Craft stall, Paderne Medieval Festival

MÚSICA PIMBA

Small-town festivals aren't complete without *música pimba*. Made for dancing, regardless of personal preferences, songs are upbeat with corny and punny lyrics, full of innuendo.

↑ LOCAL CRAFTS

Smaller events outside major urban centres are a great opportunity to see and buy local crafts as well as to sample traditional food.

▶ Discover more about traditional Portuguese crafts on p114

Best Festive Experiences

▶ Visit Óbidos in the spring for all things cacao at Festival Internacional de Chocolate (p93)

▶ Learn about the smuggling past of Alcoutim at Festival do Contrabando in the Algarve (p160)

▶ Dance to Celtic folk music in August at the Festival Intercéltico de Sendim (p232)

▶ Celebrate wine, wine and more wine at the Douro Valley's Pombaline Festival (p214)

STATE OF RULE

Portugal was a Monarchy until 5 October 1910.

On 28 May 1926 a coup instated a conservative dictatorship (*Estado Novo*).

On 25 April 1974 a military coup defeated the dictatorship (*Revolução dos Cravos*).

PIECES OF
THE PAST

Tucked between Spain and the Atlantic Ocean, rectangle-shaped Portugal has officially been a country since 1143; one of the oldest in the world. For eight centuries, and before that, a plethora of cultural influences swept the nation, creating a Portuguese identity that locals have trouble explaining. Portugal's history is complex and its past as a colonising country has shaped a future that must be reinvented. Bear witness to all the layers.

→ **COLONIAL PAST**

Wounds are fresh and far from healed. But in recent years, there's been an attempt (albeit slow) to acknowledge Portugal's colonial past.

▶ Learn more on p68

AMNAT30/SHUTTERSTOCK ©

Left Cromeleque dos Almendres, Évora
Right Slave Market Museum, Lagos
Below Convento do Carmo, Lisbon

AGE OF DISCOVERIES

Portrayed as a country of conquerors, in Portugal the so-called 'Age of Discoveries' is frequently used as the symbol of great feats.

RIGHT: KATVIC/SHUTTERSTOCK ©
LEFT: MRFOTOS/SHUTTERSTOCK ©

↑ **GREAT EARTHQUAKE**

The Great Earthquake of 1755 not only shattered Lisbon but had a profound impact on Voltaire and other key thinkers during the Age of Enlightenment.

Best Historic Experiences

▶ Visit the markers of the 1755 Great Earthquake in Lisbon (p67)

▶ Learn about Portugal's role in the slave trade at Lagos' Slave Market Museum (p160)

▶ Get in touch with the country's ancient past in Évora (p118)

▶ Explore well-preserved Iron Age settlements in Trás-os-Montes (p233)

▶ See Islamic ruins in the Alentejo town of Mértola (p111)

AGES & HOURS

The minimum legal age to drink alcohol is 18 years.

Bars generally close at around 2am to 3am.

Nightclubs typically close at the first crack of dawn, any time between 4am and 6am.

OUT ON
THE TOWN

Nights are warm in the summer and tolerably cold in the winter. If that's not a good excuse to go out on the weekends, how about affordable drinks? The working Portuguese reserve all their partying energy for Friday and Saturday nights. The habit of post-work drinks has not settled in, but on weekends late dinners turn into early nightcaps that lead to dancing until dawn.

FRÁGIL'S LEGACY

Frágil, a bar that once existed in Bairro Alto, was partially responsible for the cultural and musical awakening of 1980s Lisbon after 40-plus years of a conservative dictatorship.

Left Evening street scene, Lisbon **Right** Cocktail selection **Below** *Santos populares* celebration, Lisbon

OUTDOOR DRINKING

Grabbing a drink at the bar and joining your friends outside is standard behaviour. Weather permitting, outdoor sitting areas, if they exist, fill up fast.

▶ Join *lisboêtas* for a night on the town on p56

↑ SANTOS POPULARES

During *santos populares* in June, all etiquette rules go out the window. Porto and Lisbon streets are packed and people dance to live *música pimba*.

Best Nightlife Experiences

▶ **Bar-hop in Porto's residential Ribeira neighbourhood by day and partying hotspot by night** (p180)

▶ **Chill and toast the sunset at the Algarve's beach clubs and bars** (p151)

▶ **Paint the town pink at Lisbon's revitalised and reinvented Cais do Sodré** (p58)

WINE PARTICULARS

The Douro and the Alentejo are Portugal's largest wine-producing regions.

France, the US and the UK are the largest importers of Portuguese wine.

Vinho verde is a region, not the name of a grape or a blend.

FROM GRAPE
TO GLASS

Although the Douro Valley and the Alentejo get most of the attention, Portugal has 14 different wine regions and they cover all areas of the country. More than a drink, wine is practically a basic need and an intrinsic part of the locals' diet. With some of the oldest vineyards on earth, wine has played a key role in the country's cultural identity since Roman times.

→ REASONABLE PRICES

You can buy decent wines from supermarkets and from reputed wine producers at deliciously affordable prices. Reserve boxed wine for seasoning food and making sangria.

Left Douro Valley vineyards **Right** Wine store, Lisbon **Below** Wine with a view, Porto

WINE QUALITY

Table wine is *vinho de mesa* (basic and cheaper), then up a notch is *vinho regional*, and DOC are the wines under strict quality control.

WINE VARIETY

Follow your tastebuds to find the wine that pairs perfectly with you. You might arrive in Portugal loving reds and leave ditching them for crisp young whites.
► Learn about Portugal's *vinho verde* on p173

Best Wine Experiences

► **Explore the mighty and lush Douro Valley, for the wine and cultural experiences** (p198)

► **Taste Setúbal's sweet and fruity Moscatel** (p91)

► **Relax at a yoga class with wine at Alentejo's Adega Mayor** (p129)

► **Discover a lesser-known winemaking region in the Northeast** (p233)

► **Ensure there's port in your Portuguese adventure with a Porto lodge tour** (p184)

PORTUGAL BEST EXPERIENCES

RIVER SWIMS &
OCEAN DIPS

Half of Portugal's territory is coast, with sprawling beaches ranging from the cold and tumultuous North to the balmy and laidback South. Inland, dipping is done in crisp rivers and placid human-made reservoirs. Yearned for by locals, beach season is on everyone's agenda at the first sign of warmer days, be it an after-work quick dive or a weekend getaway with extended family and friends. August means crowds and heavy traffic.

→ **BEACH SEASON**

Officially, beach season starts on 15 June and ends 15 September. That means lifeguards are at work, not that it's beach-perfect weather.

Left Surfer, Praia do Norte, Nazaré
Right Praia do Nazaré **Below** Alqueva Dam (p111)

ACCESSIBLE BEACHES

With more than 200 accessible beaches and bathing areas, Portugal is sure to have a paddling spot that suits you to perfection.

BEACHWEAR

Beachwear is for the beach. Cover up if you need to make a quick trip to a cafe or the toilet.

Best Water Experiences

▶ **Pick one of the Alentejo's surf spots and get out on the board** (p124)

▶ **Dive in the crisp waters of human-made Azibo reservoir near Podence** (p221)

▶ **Smooth sail, deep dive or stargaze in Alqueva, Europe's largest artificial lake** (p111)

▶ **Island-hop the white sand banks of the Ria Formosa in the Algarve** (p156)

Santos Populares

During June, festivities sprout all over the country to honour the popular saints (*santos populares*) Anthony, John and Peter.

↙ Music Festivals

Dozens of events with catchy line-ups compete for attention. NOS Alive is among the most popular festivals in Europe.

📍 Lisbon

▶ nosalive.com

School's out in July and August, which means families ditch the cities for stints in the countryside or at the beach.

Day of Portugal

Portugal celebrates its national holiday on 10 June. Expect some places and attractions to be closed.

JUNE

Average daytime max: 25°C
Days of rainfall: 2 (Lisbon)

JULY

Portugal in
SUMMER

↓ Arraial Lisboa Pride

The largest LGBTIQ+ event in Portugal is a two-week-long celebration in Lisbon that ends with a parade down Avenida da Liberdade.

📍 Lisbon

▶ ilga-portugal.pt/lisboapride

With late sunsets, enjoy the outdoors as much as possible, be it exploring a park or lounging at an *esplanada*.

↑ Olhão Seafood Festival

Seafood-lovers should not miss this grand culinary fest. Highlights include regional specialities like chargrilled fish, *caldeirada* (fish stew) and *cataplana* (seafood stew).

📍 Olhão

▶ p144

☀ Average daytime max: 28°C
Days of rainfall: 0

AUGUST

☀ Average daytime max: 28°C
Days of rainfall: 1

Peak Season

Demand for accommodation peaks during summer. Book transfers, tours and overnight adventures in advance.

▶ lonelyplanet.com/portugal/activities

🧳 Packing notes

Pack a hat and sunscreen as the average UV index soars up to 10.

Check out the full calendar of events

The school year restarts in mid-September. Expect busier cities and traffic.

Republic Day

On 5 October, Portugal celebrates the start of the Republican regime. Several events take place on this national holiday.

End of the Beach Season

Beach season ends on 15 September for most of Portugal, but hot days linger. Most beaches go unguarded after this date.

⬉ Grape Harvesting Season

Between late September and early October wine regions in Portugal are bustling with harvesting activity. It's a great time to tour wineries.

SEPTEMBER

Average daytime max: 26°C
Days of rainfall: 3 (Lisbon)

OCTOBER

Portugal in
AUTUMN

October is the start of low season. With fewer crowds and lower temperatures, it can be an ideal time to visit.

↓ Although the north and the west coast can be cold and wet in November, the south and the Alentejo still get plenty of sunshine. Expect excellent prices and thin crowds.

↗ All Saints Day

1 November is a Catholic national holiday celebrating All Saints.

NOVEMBER

Average daytime max: 23°C
Days of rainfall: 8

Average daytime max: 18°C
Days of rainfall: 9

 Packing notes

Pack light options and warmer clothes to layer up, plus easy-to-carry rain gear for occasional showers.

↓ Holiday Season

Most places close on Christmas Day (25 December) and New Year's Day (1 January). Streets light up with decorations; *pastelarias* are fully stocked with seasonal sweets.

↓ Big-Wave Season

Surfers head to the beaches on the west this time of year for a chance to ride a giant wave.

National Holidays

1 and 8 December are national holidays, but most businesses are open because of holiday season.

Low season is well and truly here. Explore crowd-free landmarks and monuments, or spend time indoors in colder regions.

DECEMBER

Average daytime max: 15°C
Days of rainfall: 10 (Lisbon)

JANUARY

Portugal in
WINTER

↓ **Fantasporto**

This world-renowned two-week international festival celebrates fantasy, horror and just plain weird films.

📍 Porto

▶ fantasporto.com

↑ **Carnaval**

From traditional old pagan rituals to Brazil-inspired colourful parades, for three days (Sunday to Shrove Tuesday) most Portuguese celebrate Carnaval.

📍 Podence

▶ p232

PORTUGAL PLAN BY SEASON

Average daytime max: 15°C
Days of rainfall: 10

FEBRUARY

Average daytime max: 16°C
Days of rainfall: 8

→ **Winter flurries**

Occasional snowfall in Trás-os-Montes, close to the Spanish border.

🧳 **Packing notes**

Pack warm, waterproof clothes and footwear. Expect snow in higher places.

← Easter Holidays

Schools close for two weeks during Easter. Some families take off from urban centres for a long-weekend getaway.

↘ Nature Awakes

Spring is a great time to explore the outdoors as flowers bloom and mating season starts for most wildlife species.

It's not yet high season, but tourists from neighbouring Spain often spend the long weekend in Portugal during Easter holidays.

MARCH

Average daytime max: 18°C
Days of rainfall: 6 (Lisbon)

APRIL

Portugal in
SPRING

↘ 25 April

Liberty Day is one of the most important and widely celebrated national holidays. On this day in 1974 a military coup ended the dictatorship.

↑ Festival Internacional de Chocolate

Celebrate the sweet temptation of the cacao bean with culinary presentations by top chocolate makers and hands-on cooking activities for kids.

♥ Óbidos

▶ festivalchocolate.cm-obidos.pt

▶ p93

MAY

Average daytime max: 20°C
Days of rainfall: 7

Average daytime max: 22°C
Days of rainfall: 5

← Fátima Romarias

Hundreds of thousands make the pilgrimage to Fátima to commemorate the apparitions of the Virgin that occurred on 13 May 1917.

♥ Fátima

▶ p104

 Packing notes

Light clothes for warm afternoons; warm clothes for chilly mornings and evenings.

LISBON
Trip Builder

TAKE YOUR PICK OF MUST-SEES AND HIDDEN GEMS

■■■■ After the biting 2010–2014 financial crisis, Lisbon emerged as one of Europe's coolest cities – an achingly beautiful metropolis that combines the charm and laid-back vibe of a small town with the cosmopolitan energy of a major hub.

🗺 Trip Notes

How long Allow a week

Getting around Public transport is pretty efficient, combining a decent metro with a network of buses and picturesque tramways. The metro is most useful when venturing further afield (to the airport, for example).

Tips If you're staying within the city centre, the most efficient way to get around is on foot, provided you have good walking shoes. Lisbon's trademark mosaic sidewalks can be treacherously slippery.

Parque Eduardo VII

Pç Marquês de Pombal

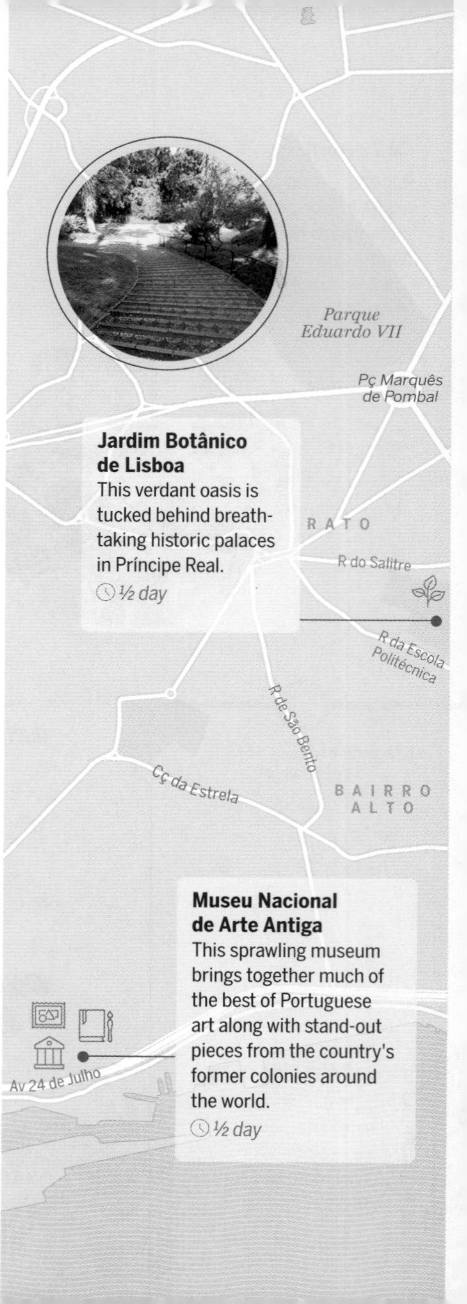

Jardim Botânico de Lisboa
This verdant oasis is tucked behind breathtaking historic palaces in Príncipe Real.
🕐 ½ day

R A T O

R do Salitre

R da Escola Politécnica

R de São Bento

Cc da Estrela

B A I R R O
A L T O

Museu Nacional de Arte Antiga
This sprawling museum brings together much of the best of Portuguese art along with stand-out pieces from the country's former colonies around the world.
🕐 ½ day

Av 24 de Julho

Museu Nacional do Azulejo

Housed in a 16th-century monastery, complete with its own gilded chapel, the Tile Museum traces this most Portuguese of art forms from its North African origins through to its heyday as a decorative way of protecting the facades of buildings.

🕐 ½ day

R Jacinta Marto

Av Fontes Pereira de Melo

Av Almirante Reis

Av Mouzinho de Albuquerque

Bairro do Avillez

Another one-stop shop bringing different restaurants – all from celebrated Portuguese chef José Avillez – under one roof.

🕐 ½ day

Av da Liberdade

R do Vale de Santo Antonio

Av Infante Dom Henrique

R O S S I O

G R A Ç A

Estação do Rossio

C A S T E L O

Cç do Combro

B A I X A

R do Alecrim

R da Alfândega

Praça do Comércio

Extending along the bank of the Tagus River, this monumental plaza feels like the gateway to the city, welcoming visitors and residents alike.

🕐 ½ day

R do Arsenal

Doca da Marinha

Cais do Sodré

Time Out Market

Ogle much of the best food the city has to offer, all under one roof. But be warned: choosing which restaurant to try can be excruciating.

🕐 ½ day

Rio Tejo

N 0 ─────── 1 km
   0 ─────── 0.5 miles

AROUND LISBON
Trip Builder

TAKE YOUR PICK OF MUST-SEES AND HIDDEN GEMS

■■■■■ Be captivated by fine sandy beaches, venture along the Tejo river banks, enjoy the local wine, and discover world heritage. For a taste of the best that Portugal has to offer, you don't even have to venture far from the capital city.

🗺 Trip Notes

Hub towns Lisbon, Sintra, Setúbal

How long Allow 7 days

Getting around There is frequent public transport such as bus or train to take you to the main destinations. If you want greater flexibility, rent a car so you can stop along the way.

Tips Avoid leaving or entering Lisbon at rush hour as you may get stuck in traffic. In high season, seaside destinations and major monuments fill up with visitors, so go early.

Colares
Visit the incredible beaches of Ursa and Adraga and stop at Cabo da Roca, the westernmost tip of continental Europe. For this trip, you will need a car.
🕐 1 day

Parque Natural de Sintra-Cascais

Praia da Adraga ☼

Praia Ursa ☼

Cabo da Roca 🗼

Sintra

Praia do Guincho ☼ **Cascais**

Atlantic Ocean

Cascais
Enjoy a round of golf overlooking the Atlantic, and then explore the village's museums and restaurants. Go to Guincho along the wooden walkways that cross the protected sand dunes.
🕐 1-2 days

ESTREMADURA

Tapada Nacional de Mafra

Mafra

Vila Franca de Xira
Discover contrasting landscapes in the Reserva Natural do Estuário do Tejo and go birdwatching in one of Portugal's most important wetlands.
🕐 *1 day*

Mafra
Visit the Palácio Nacional de Mafra, a Unesco World Heritage site. Then go for a walk in the Tapada Nacional de Mafra and see the deer.
🕐 *1-2 days*

Vila Franca de Xira 📷

Rio Tejo

Alverca do Ribatejo

Rio Sorraia

Reserva Natural do Estuário do Tejo

Rio Tejo

✪ **LISBON**

Rio Tejo

● **Almada**

Palmela
Hop between eight viewpoints in the town of Palmela and enjoy a glass of the famous regional wine.
🕐 *2 days*

Setúbal Península

Costa da Caparica
Spread your towel or have a surf session on dozens of beaches that stretch for 13km. See the gorgeous view from the top of the Arriba Fóssil.
🕐 *1 day*

● Palmela

Parque Natural da Arrábida

Ⓝ 0 ——————— 20 km
0 ——————— 10 miles

THE ALGARVE
Trip Builder

○ São Teotónio

TAKE YOUR PICK OF MUST-SEES AND HIDDEN GEMS

▬▬▬ Cliff-flanked coves, secluded sea caves and islands of golden sands decorate the coast – inviting surfers, water-sports fanatics and beachcombers. Inland, whitewashed villages and mountainous hiking trails provide a peaceful retreat.

🗺 Trip Notes

Hub towns Faro, Albufeira, Lagos

How long Allow 10 days

Getting around Hiring a car will give access to remote bays and inland villages. Trains and buses link main towns and beaches; boat trips are in abundance from tourist hubs.

Tips All beaches in the Algarve are public. Early risers will enjoy peaceful sands and calmer waters, though a quieter stretch is often only a short walk away.

Costa Vicentina & Sagres
Road trip, or hike, along the striking and lesser-visited west coast, exploring vast sands, epic surf and the dramatic cliffs of Cabo de São Vicente, mainland Portugal's most southwesterly point.
🕑 *2 days*

Serrado Monchique

Fóia ⛰

Casais ○

● **Lagos**

🥾

Sagres

Cabo de São Vicente

Lagos
Kayak through imposing sandstone towers at Ponta da Piedade before kicking back in traditional cafes and sipping cocktails in lively bars.
🕑 *1 day*

Atlantic Ocean

Ⓝ 0 — 20 km
0 — 10 miles

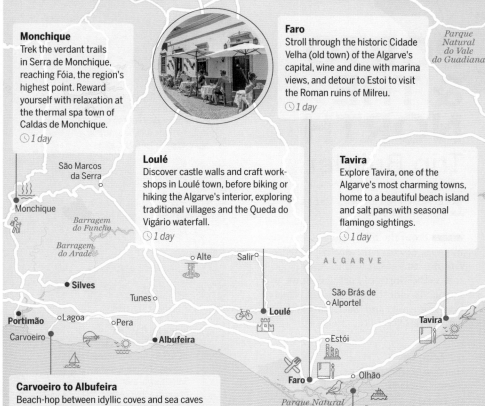

Monchique

Trek the verdant trails in Serra de Monchique, reaching Fóia, the region's highest point. Reward yourself with relaxation at the thermal spa town of Caldas de Monchique.

🕐 1 day

Faro

Stroll through the historic Cidade Velha (old town) of the Algarve's capital, wine and dine with marina views, and detour to Estoi to visit the Roman ruins of Milreu.

🕐 1 day

Parque Natural do Vale do Guadiana

São Marcos da Serra

Loulé

Discover castle walls and craft workshops in Loulé town, before biking or hiking the Algarve's interior, exploring traditional villages and the Queda do Vigário waterfall.

🕐 1 day

Tavira

Explore Tavira, one of the Algarve's most charming towns, home to a beautiful beach island and salt pans with seasonal flamingo sightings.

🕐 1 day

Monchique

Barragem do Funcho

Barragem do Arade

○ Alte   Salir ○

A L G A R V E

● **Silves**

Tunes ○

São Brás de
○ Alportel

Portimão   ○ Lagoa   ○ Pera   🚲 **Loulé**

Carvoeiro   ○ Pera

● **Albufeira**

Tavira ●

○ Estói

○ Olhão

Faro ●

Parque Natural da Ria Formosa

Carvoeiro to Albufeira

Beach-hop between idyllic coves and sea caves along this rugged stretch of coast, where water sports and boat trips to the poster-child Benagil Cave are easily accessible.

🕐 2 days

Atlantic Ocean

Olhão & Parque Natural da Ria Formosa

Pick up fresh seafood at Mercados de Olhão, take a ferry to serene islands in the Parque Natural da Ria Formosa, and admire birdlife among the dunes.

🕐 1 day

PORTO & THE NORTH

Trip Builder

TAKE YOUR PICK OF MUST-SEES AND HIDDEN GEMS

▬▬▬ From the medieval to the modern, discover the diverse visual, cultural and gastronomic tapestry that is the North of Portugal. Some of Portugal's oldest villages, most closely held traditions and least touristed spots await you here.

🗺 Trip Notes

Hub towns Porto, Peso da Régua, Valença, Guimarães

How long Allow 14 days

Getting around Hire a car to be spontaneous and let the spirit of adventure take you. Ease into the driving and take in the scenery by travelling counter-clockwise, leaving the bigger towns for the second week.

Tips In summer, save Peneda-Gerês for weekdays to avoid the weekend warriors. Forgo the expensive toll roads and take the leisurely and free national roads.

Valença
Stay in this walled border town and use it as a base for exploring the popular pilgrim stop of Ponte de Lima and other lively towns along the border with Galicia
🕐 *2 days*

Valença

Atlantic Ocean

Viana do Castelo

Viana do Castelo
Take in the spectacular view from the mountain-top site of Santuário de Santa Luzia, then head to the beaches of the Costa Verde.
🕐 *1 day*

Póvoa de Varzim

Villa do Conde

Porto

Porto
Explore Portugal's charming second city and get lost on purpose. Known as the gateway to the north, its steep historic centre will require your comfiest shoes.
🕐 *3 days*

Parque Nacional da Peneda-Gerês

Hike Portugal's only national park, a conservation area since 1971, home to wild horses and two impressive shrines (Senhora da Peneda and São Bento da Porta Aberta).

🕐 *2 days*

SPAIN

Serra da Peneda

Ponte da Barca

Parque Nacional da Peneda-Gerês

○ Montalegre

Chaves

PORTUGAL

Trás-os-Montes

Ramble the rugged landscapes and ruins of former settlements, observing a disappearing way of life in this region colloquially referred to as 'behind the mountains'.

🕐 *2 days*

Guimarães

Stay in the birthplace of Portugal, visit the castle and the historic quarter before making a side jaunt to Braga, including Bom Jesus do Monte.

🕐 *2 days*

Braga

Guimarães ●

Vila Nova de Famalicão

●**Mirandela**

Parque Natural do Alvão

Valqueiro △

●**Vila Real**

Rio Tua

●**Amarante**

● **Penafiel**

Peso da Régua ●

Rio Douro

○ Tua

Parque Natural do Douro Internacional

Douro Valley

Unwind at the estates of the wine region while brushing up on your oenology, and tap into your inner archaeologist at the prehistoric sites of Parque Côa.

🕐 *2 days*

0 — **50 km**
0 — **25 miles**

ALONG THE COAST
Trip Builder

TAKE YOUR PICK OF MUST-SEES AND HIDDEN GEMS

■■■ Fishing and shellfish-gathering traditions are in their origins, but these seaside towns are increasingly on surfers' radars. Here, the seafood is just-off-the-boat fresh, the cliffs are rugged and wild, and the waves are magnificently challenging.

🗺 Trip Notes

Hub towns Lisbon, Caldas da Rainha, Leiria

How long Allow 5 days

Getting around Rent a car and explore the coastal area at your own pace. If you decide to use public transport, be aware that you will probably have to make several transfers before you reach your destination.

Tips Opt for the roads along the coastline. It will certainly take longer, but the scenery is more pleasant, and you will save on highway tolls.

Atlantic Ocean

Foz do Arelho
Explore the wooden walkways that run along the cliffs of Foz do Arelho. Stand-up paddle-board or kayak in the calm waters of the Lagoa de Óbidos.
🕐 *1 day*

Reserva Natural das Berlengas

Santa Cruz
Walk along this extensive sandy beach and marvel at the cliffs of Ponta da Vigia, and the Penedo do Guincho.
🕐 *half-day*

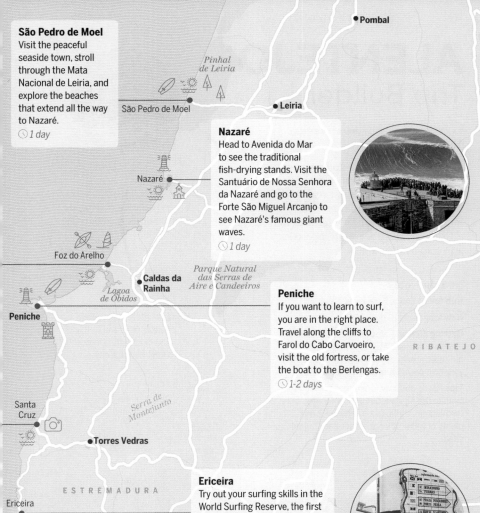

São Pedro de Moel
Visit the peaceful seaside town, stroll through the Mata Nacional de Leiria, and explore the beaches that extend all the way to Nazaré.
🕓 *1 day*

São Pedro de Moel

Pinhal de Leiria

• **Pombal**

• **Leiria**

Nazaré
Head to Avenida do Mar to see the traditional fish-drying stands. Visit the Santuário de Nossa Senhora da Nazaré and go to the Forte São Miguel Arcanjo to see Nazaré's famous giant waves.
🕓 *1 day*

Nazaré •

Foz do Arelho •

Caldas da Rainha

Lagoa de Óbidos

Parque Natural das Serras de Aire e Candeeiros

Peniche

Peniche
If you want to learn to surf, you are in the right place. Travel along the cliffs to Farol do Cabo Carvoeiro, visit the old fortress, or take the boat to the Berlengas.
🕓 *1-2 days*

R I B A T E J O

Santa Cruz

Serra de Montejunto

• **Torres Vedras**

E S T R E M A D U R A

Ericeira
Try out your surfing skills in the World Surfing Reserve, the first in Europe. Go for a walk in the picturesque village and sample the fresh fish or seafood in one of the many local restaurants.
🕓 *1-2 days*

Ericeira

Parque Natural de Sintra-Cascais

Rio Tejo

LISBON ✪

◉ 0 ── 40 km
  0 ──────── 20 miles

ALENTEJO
Trip Builder

**TAKE YOUR PICK OF MUST-SEES
AND HIDDEN GEMS**

▰▰▰ Oak trees lost in golden prairies come to mind when you speak of the Alentejo, Portugal's largest region. But this is also a land of hilltop castles, hidden beaches, fruitful vineyards and artisans creating beautiful tapestries and colourful ceramics.

📖 Trip Notes

Hub towns Évora, Beja, Elvas, Sines

How long Allow 10 days

Getting around Trains and buses connect Lisbon with major Alentejo cities, but hiring a car will get you much further at your own pace; tours are also an option.

Tips Roads are busy in summer, as people head to the Algarve, but when exiting the Alentejo, traffic fades. If hiking, bring plenty of water: it's not always easy to find shade.

Río Tejo

Arraiolos
Admire the hand-woven rugs that fill the streets and visit the circular castle on the outskirts.
🕓 ½ day

Montemor-o-Novo ●

Évora
Explore Neolithic sites, Roman ruins and Gothic churches in this Unesco World Heritage city.
🕓 1 day

*Atlantic
Ocean*

Sines ●

Porto Côvo ●

B A I X O
A L E N T E J O

Porto Covo
Put your surfing skills to the test and sample seafood platters in this charming beach town. It's also the perfect starting point for hiking the Rota Vicentina, one of Europe's best coastal trails.
🕓 1-2 days

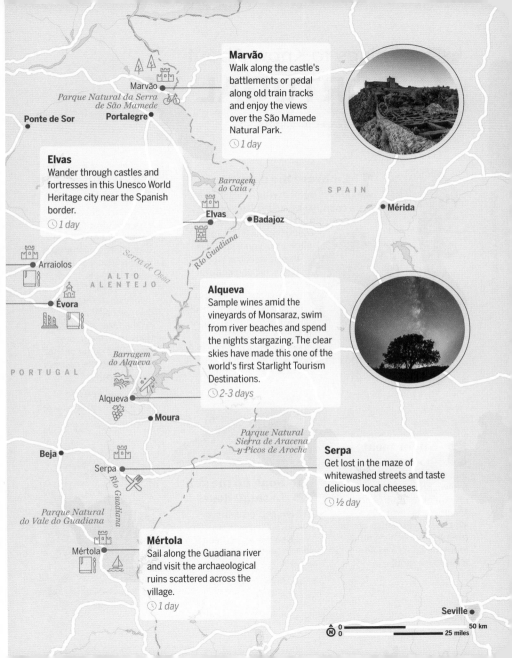

Marvão
Walk along the castle's battlements or pedal along old train tracks and enjoy the views over the São Mamede Natural Park.
🕐 1 day

Parque Natural da Serra de São Mamede

Ponte de Sor

Marvão

Portalegre

Elvas
Wander through castles and fortresses in this Unesco World Heritage city near the Spanish border.
🕐 1 day

Barragem do Caia

Elvas

Badajoz

SPAIN

Mérida

Arraiolos

Serra de Ossa

ALTO ALENTEJO

Río Guadiana

Évora

Alqueva
Sample wines amid the vineyards of Monsaraz, swim from river beaches and spend the nights stargazing. The clear skies have made this one of the world's first Starlight Tourism Destinations.
🕐 2-3 days

Barragem do Alqueva

PORTUGAL

Alqueva

Moura

Parque Natural Sierra de Aracena y Picos de Aroche

Serpa
Get lost in the maze of whitewashed streets and taste delicious local cheeses.
🕐 ½ day

Beja

Serpa

Río Guadiana

Parque Natural do Vale do Guadiana

Mértola

Mértola
Sail along the Guadiana river and visit the archaeological ruins scattered across the village.
🕐 1 day

Seville

0 — 50 km
0 — 25 miles
Ⓝ

7 Things to Know About
PORTUGAL

INSIDER TIPS TO HIT THE GROUND RUNNING

1 Embrace the detours

At first sight, Portugal might seem like a country easy to fully explore in a matter of weeks. But no matter how well you plan the time you'll spend on the ground, the local historical and cultural richness, intriguing and mixed cuisine, and the people you meet will most likely have you chasing an off-the-map adventure. Go with the flow, Portuguese-style, and embrace the detours.

2 Portuguese is not Spanish

Most Portuguese, especially younger people, are fairly fluent in one foreign language. Near the border, locals will most likely speak fluent Spanish. That said, even though no one will call you out on the faux pas, don't think both languages sound the same or that everyone in the country speaks both.

▶ Discover Portugal's second official language on p222

3 Sit for meals

Grabbing a quick bite is rare and most likely a product of an unexpected emergency. Mealtime is normally a sit-down experience at the table, whether you're lunching solo or meeting friends for dinner.

4 Soak up the sun in small doses

On average, Portugal has around 300 days of sunshine a year, so there's no need to get it all under your skin in one go.

▶ See more about the seasons on p22

5 A young democracy

Portugal's democracy is barely 50 years old. Some wounds remain very exposed still: the country's colonial past; five decades of an ultra-conservative dictatorship; the political prisoners that faced torture and persecution. As Portugal reckons with its past, there is an effort now to open up to much-needed, albeit difficult, conversations. The process is ongoing, but slow.

6 Slang & regional dialects

Some Portuguese expressions don't actually mean what they say, which can make communication misfire (without any unrepairable consequences, though). Unofficial contractions that aren't part of any grammar book don't make it easier, either. Here are a few examples:

tudo bem? – more of an end-all phrase than an actual expression of concern from the person asking how you are

então – a flexible word that changes meaning at each inflection. It can be a short form of a concerned question or a replacement for 'hello' (então?), a polite 'watch it' (então!), or a pause someone makes before starting a lengthy explanation (então...)

t'fona-me – a super-contracted short form for *telefona-me* (call me), mainly used in the Greater Lisbon area

In addition, regional dialects make the language even more colourful (and challenging), like the penchant for Northerners to replace the v with b (*vaca*, Portuguese for cow, becomes *baca*, for example).

▶ See the Language chapter on p248

▶ See the Language chapter on p248

PORTUGAL LOCAL TIPS

7 Kissing strangers

The Portuguese are friendly and welcoming and, in a pre-Covid-19 world, reserved handshakes for professional encounters. Women meeting friends or being introduced to someone for the first time were greeted with a quick kiss on each cheek. Men shook hands, sometimes elaborately. Hugging involved a more intimate relationship. In a post-Covid-19 world, who knows? Perhaps a greeting will just be a smile and a wave...

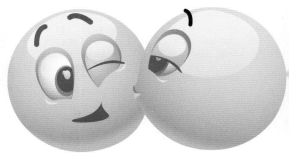

Read, Listen, Watch & Follow

READ

The Book of Disquiet (Fernando Pessoa/Bernardo Soares; 1982) Unedited pieces of text published posthumously.

A Short Book on the Great Earthquake (Rui Tavares; 2020) The events that shook Lisbon on 1 November 1755.

Journey to Portugal (José Saramago; 1990) Tales of cultural discovery while travelling through Portugal.

Escape Goat (2020) A serial novel written by 46 contemporary Portuguese authors during the Covid-19 pandemic.

LISTEN

Excuse Me (Salvador Sobral; 2016) Debut album of the jazz and soul singer who (surprisingly) won the Eurovision Song Contest in 2017.

Encore (Capicua; 2021) Porto-based Portuguese rapper and hip-hop musician launched this EP featuring her last concerts performed in 2020 before the Covid-19 lockdown.

Mariza Canta Amália (Mariza; 2020) Fado singer Mariza (pictured right) pays tribute to the genre's diva with a record celebrating her best songs.

Wolfheart (Moonspell; 1995) The debut album that propelled the gothic metal band into fame, both nationally and internationally.

Lisboa Mulata (Dead Combo; 2011) The band's instrumental rock-and-blues-fusion fourth album pays tribute to Lisbon's multicultural diversity.

▷ WATCH

Belarmino (Fernando Lopes; 1964) This docufiction follows former boxer Belarmino and symbolises the birth of Cinema Novo in Portugal.

Lisbon Story (Wim Wenders; 1994; pictured right) Drama/musical shot in Lisbon, featuring former Madredeus' lead singer Teresa Salgueiro.

Vitalina Varela (Pedro Costa; 2019) Drama feature film where Cape Verdean Vitalina Varela plays a fictionalised version of herself.

Os Filhos do Rock (Pedro Varela; 2013) TV show inspired by Portugal's 1980s rock-music generation.

Capitães de Abril (Maria de Medeiros; 2000) Story of how the peaceful military coup overthrew the dictatorship in 1974.

UNITED ARCHIVES/GETTY IMAGES ©

◎ FOLLOW

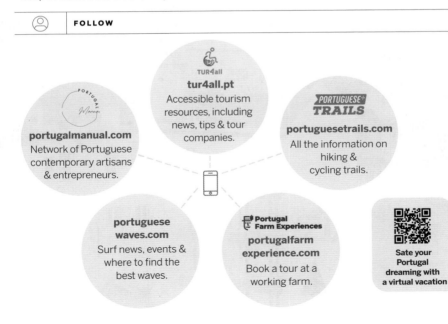

tur4all.pt
Accessible tourism resources, including news, tips & tour companies.

portugalmanual.com
Network of Portuguese contemporary artisans & entrepreneurs.

PORTUGUESE TRAILS
portuguesetrails.com
All the information on hiking & cycling trails.

portuguese waves.com
Surf news, events & where to find the best waves.

Portugal Farm Experiences
portugalfarm experience.com
Book a tour at a working farm.

Sate your Portugal dreaming with a virtual vacation

LISBON

CHILL | CHARMING | OLD SCHOOL

Experience
Lisbon
online

Bonus Online Experiences
- **Art Hits the Streets**

- **Rotating Taps**

LISBON
Trip Builder

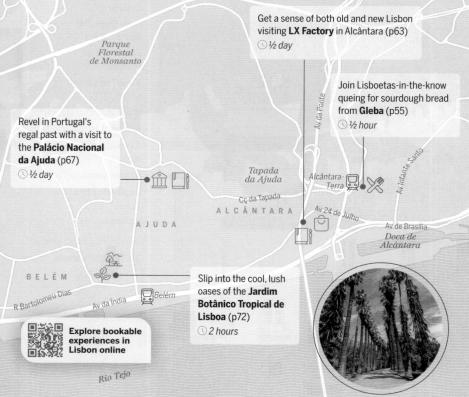

In one of Europe's coolest metropolises, soak up the pastel cityscape over a glass of wine at a hilltop park, examine the city's remarkable but fraught history, and delve into a nightlife scene that fuses Brazilian and African beats along with homegrown musical traditions.

Get a sense of both old and new Lisbon visiting **LX Factory** in Alcântara (p63)
🕓 ½ day

Join Lisboetas-in-the-know queing for sourdough bread from **Gleba** (p55)
🕓 ½ hour

Revel in Portugal's regal past with a visit to the **Palácio Nacional da Ajuda** (p67)
🕓 ½ day

Slip into the cool, lush oases of the **Jardim Botânico Tropical de Lisboa** (p72)
🕓 2 hours

Parque Florestal de Monsanto

Av da Ponte

Tapada da Ajuda

Cç da Tapada

ALCÂNTARA

Alcântara-Terra

Av Infante Santo

Av 24 de Julho

Av de Brasília

Doca de Alcântara

AJUDA

BELÉM

R Bartolomeu Dias

Av da Índia

Belém

Rio Tejo

Explore bookable experiences in Lisbon online

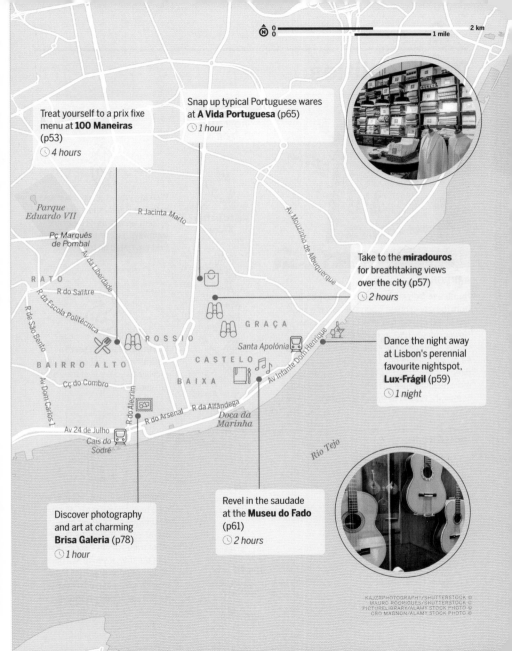

Treat yourself to a prix fixe menu at **100 Maneiras** (p53)
🕐 *4 hours*

Snap up typical Portuguese wares at **A Vida Portuguesa** (p65)
🕐 *1 hour*

Take to the **miradouros** for breathtaking views over the city (p57)
🕐 *2 hours*

Dance the night away at Lisbon's perennial favourite nightspot, **Lux-Frágil** (p59)
🕐 *1 night*

Revel in the saudade at the **Museu do Fado** (p61)
🕐 *2 hours*

Discover photography and art at charming **Brisa Galeria** (p78)
🕐 *1 hour*

Parque Eduardo VII

Pç Marquês de Pombal

R A T O

R do Salitre

Av. da Liberdade

R da Escola Politécnica

R de São Bento

B A I R R O   A L T O

Av. Dom Carlos 1

Cç do Combro

R do Alecrim

Av 24 de Julho

Cais do Sodré

R Jacinta Marto

Av. Mouzinho de Albuquerque

R O S S I O

G R A Ç A

Santa Apolónia

C A S T E L O

B A I X A

Av. Infante Dom Henrique

R do Arsenal

R da Alfândega

Doca da Marinha

Rio Tejo

0 — 1 mile
0 — 2 km

Practicalities

ARRIVING

Humberto Delgado Airport Located just 7km from the city centre, Lisbon's airport is a short and cheap cab or Uber ride, or even cheaper but slower subway ride, from the main neighbourhoods of interest. The subway, which costs just €1.50 for a single-ride ticket, is located almost directly beneath Terminal 1, which is used by most major airlines. (The bleak, warehouse-like Terminal 2 is used by low-cost carriers.)

HOW MUCH FOR A

Galão (latte)
€1.50

Wine at a
kiosk €3

Round of Azeitão
cheese €4

GETTING AROUND

Walking While the city does have a decent – and expanding – metro system, as well as its hallmark tramways, Lisbon is indisputably best navigated on foot.

Subway Doesn't yet serve all the central neighbourhoods, but is excellent if you're venturing a bit further afield.

WHEN TO GO

JAN–MAR
Chilly and sometimes rainy; a good time to avoid the crowds

APR–JUN
Longer, brighter days and warmer weather

JUL–SEP
High tourist season means an influx of visitors

OCT–DEC
The rainiest months of the year

Tramway The iconic 28E tramway runs from Mouraria to Campo de Ourique and can get quite crowded, but there are several other tram lines in Lisbon. Don't take the tram if you're in a hurry, as it's not uncommon for them to get trapped behind a poorly parked car or other obstacle.

EATING & DRINKING

Bacalhau à Brás While there are scores of ways to serve *bacalhau* (salted cod), this tasty mixture of shredded cod with onions, potatoes and scrambled eggs is particularly beloved by Lisboetas.

Moscatel Produced on the Setúbal Peninsula, just south of Lisbon, this fortified wine gives Porto a run for its money.

Ginja Often served in small chocolate cups, this dessert liqueur made from cherries is the drink of choice in Lisbon's Alfama neighbourhood.

Must-try gelato	Best bread
Gelato Davvero (p77)	Gleba (p55)

CONNECT & FIND YOUR WAY

Wi-fi Most European mobile phone plans generally include data roaming in Portugal. For those without a European plan, it's worth getting a SIM card on a prepaid plan from one of the country's three operators: Vodafone, MEO or NOS.

Navigation With its narrow winding streets, Lisbon is hard to navigate without the help of a navigation app.

WHERE TO STAY

Central Lisbon is fairly compact, meaning that you can move easily from one neighbourhood to the next.

Neighbourhood	Atmosphere
Alfama	This dense warren of little streets is among Lisbon's most picturesque areas, and its most popular.
Bairro Alto	Lisbon's party central, this is the place to be if going out is your main focus.
Chiado	This gorgeous central neighbourhood is among the city's chicest and most expensive.
Campo de Ourique	A bit further out, this neighbourhood offers many of the advantages of Chiado at a lower price.
Arroios	This once rough neighbourhood now offers one of the best quality-to-price ratios in the city.

SENSIBLE SHOES

Be sure to wear shoes with grippy soles, as Lisbon's mosaic sidewalks – known as *calçada portuguesa* – are slippery, and injuries are not uncommon.

MONEY

Carry cash – preferably small notes – as some restaurants still don't accept cards, and getting change for bigger notes is a perennial problem.

01 Eating
LISBON

FRESH | AUTHENTIC | DIVERSE

▬▬▬ Restaurants in Lisbon run the gamut from the simplest *tascas* (traditional Portuguese bistros), where both the decor and the prices appear untouched by the passage of time, to erstwhile palaces that serve up Michelin-starred delicacies. And whether you're paying €7 or €200, one thing is for sure: that seafood you're being served is fresh. In Lisbon, frozen fish is practically heresy.

ILPO MUSTO / ALAMY STOCK PHOTO ©

🗺 How to

Not all restaurants accept cards Play it safe by going out armed with cash.

The early bird gets the dinner worm Many *tascas* don't accept reservations; to avoid long queues, it can be a good idea to arrive early.

Appetisers aren't free! Tuck into that spread that's been laid out on the table, and you may find a steep fee tacked on to your bill. Send them back untouched if you don't want them.

BESTRAVELVIDEO/SHUTTERSTOCK ©

SALVADOR AZNAR/SHUTTERSTOCK ©

Left Al fresco dining, Chiado neighbourhood **Far left top** José Avillez' Belcanto restaurant **Far left bottom** Grilled sardines

LISBON EXPERIENCES

Long dominated by family-run *tascas*, Lisbon's food scene has undergone a renaissance over the past decade as a new generation of young chefs elevate Portuguese staples to new heights of sophistication.

'The change is gigantic,' said Ljubomir Stanisic, the chef behind the Michelin-starred restaurant 100 Maneiras and its more casual sister, Bistro 100 Maneiras. 'We've really begun to valorise our local products and traditions.'

Fine dining With its newly minted Michelin star, awarded in 2020, **100 Maneiras** leads the pack of Lisbon's fine-dining establishments. The restaurant's inventive (and photogenic) tasting menu playfully incorporates the culinary traditions of Stanisic's native Bosnia and his adopted homeland. Another Michelin-starred option is **Belcanto**, the jewel in the crown of chef and restaurateur José Avillez, who is also behind a host of other favourites, including **Pizzaria Lisboa** and **Bairro do Avillez**.

Tascas These unassuming restaurants serve up multi-course meals that are often so much more than the sum of their simple parts – often for as little as €7. A solid choice is **A Casa da Índia**, which boasts classic Portuguese fare at affordable prices.

Vegans & vegetarians While Portuguese food is heavy on the animal products, Lisbon's vegan and vegetarian offerings have mushroomed (pun intended!) in recent years. Favourites include **Ao 26 Vegan Food Project**, known for its meatless burgers, and **Psi**, which specialises in Asian-influenced fare.

🥣 Lisbon's Culinary Scene

Lisbon has a very vibrant and interesting culinary scene that's on par with any major European capital. Within a small radius, you can find everything from traditional *tascas* with honest prices to fine Portuguese dining to great international food – all made with excellent ingredients that are treated with the care and respect they deserve. Over the past decade, we've seen a real consolidation of our identity. There's a whole crop of young chefs who are bringing a real contemporary vision to Portuguese cuisine.

Ljubomir Stanisic, *chef at 100 Maneiras, one of the city's most acclaimed restaurants.* @ljubostanisic

BRUNO GIF RIBEIRO/SHUTTERSTOCK ©

Portuguese Cuisine

HOMELY AND WORLDLY, BOTH AT THE SAME TIME

The words 'Portuguese cuisine' tend to conjure up hardy rural fare, like an artfully grilled fish on a bed of varied starches. But while there is some truth in the stereotype – who can argue with a freshly grilled sardine? – Portuguese food is so much more than that.

From Portugal to the World (& Back)

The understated complexity underpinning Portuguese cuisine is perhaps best encapsulated in three little-known facts: not only was it the Portuguese who first introduced tea to England, but they also are at least partly responsible for the fieriness of much of Indian food, having ferried the chilli – a native of Latin America – to the subcontinent. As if that weren't enough, the Portuguese are also behind tempura, Japan's answer to the Portuguese batter-fried green beans known as *peixinhos da horta*, which literally translates as 'garden fishies'.

Portugal's seafaring tradition not only helped influence the culinary evolution of such far-flung cultures, but also meant that the flavours of those distant places have enriched Portuguese food.

Traditional Pastries

Take, for example, Portuguese pastries, known as *doces conventuais* or 'convent sweets' after the 16th-century nuns who consumed a prodigious amount of egg whites to starch their habits and started churning out custardy sweets as a way of keeping the yolks from going to waste. At a time when most of Europe was still relying on honey as a sweetener, the Portuguese were already receiving shipments of 'white gold' – sugar – from its colony in Brazil. (Along with egg yolks, sugar is the crucial ingredient in *doces conventuais*, which include *barriga de freira*, *broas de ovos-moles* and *toucinho-do-céu*, as well as the wildly popular *pastéis de Belém*, otherwise known as *pastéis de nata*).

Left *Peixinhos da horta* **Middle** *Doces conventuais* **Right** Sardines grilling for *santos populares*

Salted Cod

The single most prevalent ingredient in Portuguese cuisine – *bacalhau*, or salted cod – also found its way to Portugal via seafaring. Cod is native to the frigid waters off Norway and Newfoundland, and the Vikings were the first to turn this fish into a non-perishable by drying it – thanks to Portuguese salt. The perfect food for Portuguese navigators' months-long transoceanic journeys, salted cod would soon become a staple of the Portuguese diet, served up in uncounted iterations.

> At a time when most of Europe was still relying on honey as a sweetener, the Portuguese were already receiving shipments of 'white gold' – sugar – from its colony in Brazil.

Other types of seafood are also central to Portuguese cuisine – so much so, in fact, that the country has the world's third-highest per capita consumption of seafood, after Korea and Norway.

Sardines

Sardines are another fishy favourite, especially during the *santos populares*, the annual street parties ostensibly celebrating Lisbon's (technically unofficially but widely embraced) patron saint, Santo António. Every June, Lisbon's air grows thick and pungent with the inescapable scent of sardines being grilled over open-air barbecues set up on sidewalks as neighbours congregate in raucous block parties.

⊘ Gleba

This unusual bakery is among the most phenomenal success stories to sweep Lisbon's food scene in years, with legions of devoted fans who queue up for baker and entrepreneur Diogo Amorim's crunchy sourdough spheres.

Aged just 21 when he started Gleba in 2017, Amorim is dedicated to traditional breads made exclusively from Portuguese-grown cereals – a revolutionary conceit in a country where 90% of the flour is made from imported grains.

'The hardest part was to find farmers who still grow traditional varieties of wheat, rye and corn,' said Amorim, who mills all the grains on site.

02 From Dusk TILL DAWN

CHILL | FAR-FLUNG | HEARTFELT

Lisbon's trademark laid-back attitude extends to its nightlife. While the stakes are definitely lower here than in some other European capitals, Lisbon has something for almost everyone, from a club where some of the world's top DJ spin to intimate venues serving up wildly eclectic tunes.

FINN STOCK/SHUTTERSTOCK ©

📱 How to

Getting around
Because central Lisbon is so small and safe, bar-hopping is best done on foot.

When to go While the Portuguese are not as extreme night owls as their Spanish neighbours, venues in Lisbon close relatively late, at around 3am or 4am for bars and 6am for clubs.

Watch the footwear
If you plan to check out multiple bars, wear shoes that can handle the mosaic sidewalks (not heels!).

VERONICKA/SHUTTERSTOCK ©

A typical *lisboêta* night out often involves several very different types of experiences, rolled into one. For a perfect start, watch the sunset over a glass of Portuguese wine in one of the many *miradouros* (lookouts), the parks and plazas perched atop Lisbon's myriad hills that boast enviable views over the pastel cityscape. (Legend has it the city was originally built atop seven hills, but a few days of hoofing it up and down the city's seemingly endless peaks and valleys will suffice to make it feel as if the hills number in the hundreds!)

TRABANTOS/SHUTTERSTOCK ©

Old-school charm Take a dip into the Lisbon of old with a cocktail at one of the charming historic bars, their interiors apparently un-touched for decades. In Príncipe Real, try the **Pavilhão Chinês**, its walls lined with a diz-zying array of artfully displayed old objects,

🏃 Lisbon Nightlife

Lisbon may be a small city, but the whole world is here. There's also a huge diversity in the type of experiences available here – with the simplest and most humble venues to the most sophisti-cated ones.

Mikas, *owner of the Social B bar. @socialb_lisboa*

Left Miradouro da Graça
Above left Evening streetscape, Lisbon
Above right Yellow and red sangria

or the red-velvet-swathed **Foxtrot**. **Pensão Amor**, a brothel-turned-bar in the former red-light district and now nightlife-hotspot Cais do Sodré, is another great option.

Cais do Sodré In the Cais do Sodré district, your choices multiply vertiginously. In the mood for live music? Perfect. But what kind of music? **B.Leza** serves up live Brazilian and African tunes in a raucous, crowded, club-like setting. For similarly eclectic offerings in a much more intimate space, try **Tejo Bar,** a

musicians' favourite where many of the sets seem to bubble up spontaneously, and the bargoers show their appreciation – and their respect for the neighbours – not by clapping but rather by rubbing their hands together silently. While fado is sometimes on offer at Tejo Bar, to be sure you don't miss out on the quintessential *lisboêta* musical style, head to **Casa de Linhares**, which none other than the queen of pop herself, Madonna, was known to frequent in the three or so years

🍸 **Mikas' Favourites**

Here are some of nightlife empresario Mikas' favourite spots for a night out:

For drinks Mikas' own natural wine bar, Sikam, and another of his former projects, A Tabacaria, a sophisticated cocktail bar named after the tobacco shop that this tiny space housed in its previous incarnation.

For clubbing Jamaica – Mikas has long been a fan of this fixture of Pink Street, a formerly seedy stretch in Cais do Sodré that became a nightlife hub after bar and club owners successfully lobbied city officials to close the street to traffic and paint the asphalt pink.

Recommended by Mikas, *owner of the Social B bar* @socialb_lisboa

Left A Tabacaria **Below** Pavilhão Chinês (p57)

that she and her family called Lisbon home. While most *casas de fado* offer a prix fixe meal that includes the show, at most you can also sneak into the bar after the meal service to revel in the gut-wrenching spectacle over a glass of wine.

Big night out Night owls can make the evening last by heading to one of the neighbourhood's clubs. Top choices include **Musicbox**, which has hiphop nights, and **Incógnito**, a favourite for indie-music lovers. **Lux-Frágil**, which offers revellers the choice of different types of music on different floors, as well as an outsized terrace, has long held the title of Lisbon's top club, regularly attracting some of the world's biggest-name DJs.

The Sound of Longing

MUSIC THAT PLUMBS THE PORTUGUESE SOUL

When singer Amália Rodrigues died in 1999, Portugal's prime minister declared three days of national mourning. It's hard to envisage another performer commanding such a grand final gesture, but over her 50-year career, Rodrigues had grown into an uncontested national treasure – a living symbol of one the most uniquely Portuguese of art forms: fado.

Left Fado performers, Alfama **Middle** Amália Rodrigues concert poster **Right** Museu do Fado

Widely compared to Spain's national music, flamenco, fado is darker, rawer and more heartrending than its raucous Spanish cousin. It's also regarded by many Portuguese as a melodic embodiment to the often-brooding and melancholic national character. Traditionally consisting of a single, usually female, singer accompanied by a 12-string Portuguese guitar, fado plumbs the depths of what the Portuguese refer to as *saudade* – a feeling that Portuguese speakers almost defiantly insist has no precise English translation but is essentially an amalgam of homesickness, yearning, sadness and resignation. What fado lacks in upbeat cheer, it makes up for in depth of feeling.

Emerging in the early 19th century in the riverside neighbourhoods of central Lisbon, fado was initially the music of the disenfranchised – of pimps and sex workers, petty criminals and day labourers, and also of the sailors from the world over who dropped anchor in the city. It gradually grew in popularity and moved out of brothels and flophouses and into more 'respectable' venues. With the 1926 military coup that ushered in the authoritarian dictatorship of António Salazar, fado became increasingly institutionalised, with a fixed repertoire and performances in so-called *casas de fado* (fado houses), many of them concentrated in Lisboa's Bairro Alto and some of which are still around today. Because it had been embraced by Salazar, whose slogan was Deus, Pátria, e Família (God, Country, and Family), fado would be widely rejected by younger generations following the near-bloodless 1974 Carnation Revolution that brought the nearly half-century-long regime to an end.

Where to Revel in the Saudade

For a deeper dive into the history of fado, check out the Museu do Fado, in Alfama, which traces its emergence as the quintessential Portuguese musical genre. Chock-a-block with fado-related memorabilia, the museum makes for a good preamble to some of the nearby *casas de fado*. There are literally dozens of such venues, some more authentic, upscale or kitsch than others. Among the most prestigious is the Mesa de Frades (Rua dos Remédios 139), where some of the most acclaimed contemporary fado acts perform regularly.

> Fado was initially the music of the disenfranchised – of pimps and sex workers, petty criminals and day labourers, and of the sailors from the world over who dropped anchor in the city.

Fado Today

Largely eschewed by Baby Boomers, who were on the front lines of the Carnation Revolution, fado has been embraced by successive generations, and now top performers and fans make up a diverse group that includes many with roots in Portugal's former colonies. This new generation of *fadistas*, who include the Grammy-nominated singer Mariza, has injected a stiff dose of innovation and experimentation, pushing the envelope of traditional fado by incorporating a diverse array of instruments and musical influences. Many of these new *fadistas* have also pushed back against the sober black costumes and are taking to the stage in colourful, exuberant and even, gasp, occasionally sexy looks.

Casas de Fado

Adega Machado A fixture of the Bairro Alto since 1937, it's a favourite of hardcore fado fans.

O Faia Another top *casa de fado* in the Bairro Alto, O Faia has played host to many of the biggest names in fado, past and present.

Senhor Vinho A much newer addition to the fado scene – it was founded in 1975 – Senhor Vinho is the night owls' favourite, with its kitchen that stays open till midnight.

Clube de Fado This former stable a stone's throw away from the Sé Cathedral is another reliable purveyor of authentic fado.

03

Stroll the Lisbon
OF OLD

RETRO | AUTHENTIC | HIP

▬▬▬ While Lisbon has busily set about reinventing itself since it emerged as a hot tourist destination over the past few years, much of the city's appeal resides in its old-school charm – which lives on, largely undisturbed, in Alcântara.

RIBEIROANTONIO/SHUTTERSTOCK ©

🗺 Trip Notes

Getting here Take the 15E tram, which leaves from the central Praça da Figueira and extends all the way to the far-western neighborhood of Algés.

When to go Because the beauty of this place lies in its exquisite ordinariness, any old day is a good one to visit!

History Once exurban farmland, Alcântara was eventually absorbed into Lisbon and later became a textiles hub before succumbing to the privation of deindustrialization. Shielded by a rough reputation, Alcântara largely avoided the recent wave of gentrification, making it the perfect place to take in the Lisbon of old.

📖 Saving History

'Lisbon is a unique, historic city. But it's changing so fast,' notes Helena Espvall, who has spearheaded a campaign to save a crumbling 19th-century mansion on her street, Rua dos Lusíadas, which was slated to be turned into a hotel.

Helena Espvall,
a Swedish-born musician and Alcântara resident.
@helenaespvall

02 This industrial complex once housed a printing press and a textile plant but now **LX Factory** is a buzzing hive of clothing and jewellery stores, co-working spaces, bookshops, and hip restaurants and bars.

03 Get a taste of the Alentejo region at **Solar dos Nunes**, a high-end, family-run restaurant that has been written up in the *Michelin Guide* and has garnered a celebrity clientele, including Madonna.

Parque Florestal de Monsanto

Tapada da Ajuda

Tapada das Necessidades

L A P A

Av da Ponte

Av de Ceuta

Av Infante Santo

Alcântara-Terra

Cç da Tapada

R dos Lusíadas

R Primeiro de Maio

Av 24 de Julho

R Presidente Arriaga

04 Built in 1549, **Capela de Santo Amaro** (pictured left) has fantastic tile work and, perched atop a hill, offers a privileged view out over the Tagus and the nearby Ponte 25 de Abril – Lisbon's answer to the Golden Gate Bridge.

A L C Â N T A R A

Alcântara-Mar

Doca de Alcântara

Doca de Santo Amaro

Av da Índia

Ponte 25 de Abril

Rio Tejo

05 For a closer look at the Ponte 25 de Abril from 80m above ground, and to be wowed by this feat of engineering, check out **Experiência Pilar 7**.

01 Start the tour just outside the eastern edge of Alcântara, in Lapa, at the unmissable **Museu Nacional de Arte Antiga**. Housed in a 17th-century palace, the museum has an unbeatable collection of Portuguese art, as well as treasures from former colonies from Brazil to Japan.

N

0   1 km
0   0.5 miles

04 Made in
PORTUGAL

HANDCRAFTED | QUALITY | OLD-SCHOOL

Portugal is one of the last remaining enclaves of artisanal savoir faire in Europe. Here, you can still find craftspeople making everything from ceramics and leather goods to baskets, hand-spun wool and furniture the old way – according to traditional, or even millennial, techniques.

INGEHOGENBIJL/SHUTTERSTOCK ©

🗺 **How to**

Seek out artisans Outdoor fairs that are often held in parks are a great place to connect with local makers.

Carry cash Otherwise you might find yourself searching for an ATM.

Out for lunch Some stores, particularly small family-run shops, still follow the Old World tradition of closing during lunchtime, and some are only open until around noon on Saturdays.

GREG ELMS/LONELY PLANET ©

Left A Vida Portuguesa **Far left top** Portuguese ceramics **Far left bottom** Feira da Ladra

A Vida Portuguesa

Major international fashion labels come to Portugal to source the kind of handiwork that is nearly impossible to find elsewhere. Give those brands a miss and head straight to A Vida Portuguesa, a one-stop-shop for all things Made In Portugal. Among Lisbon's coolest and most unique shops, it brings together some of the best handicrafts from around the country along with quintessentially old-school Portuguese brands whose products and packaging have remained unchanged for decades. It might sound kitsch, and probably would actually be if everything weren't so appealingly curated and artfully displayed.

The store's two Lisbon locations are both so perfect that you can't help but want to snap up just about everything. Never imagined that you needed a cabbage-leaf-shaped soup bowl by the storied Portuguese ceramics maker **Bordalo Pinheiro**, or a pair of hand-tooled leather clogs, or silver polish that comes in the most fetching little metal tin? Not until you walk into A Vida Portuguesa. Also, be sure not miss the store's selection of fancy soaps and perfumes from **Claus Porto**, the historic soap maker, which also has its own standalone store on Rua da Miséricordia.

🏚 Feira da Ladra

There's no end to the treasures on offer at the Feira da Ladra (which literally – and appropriately – translates as Thieves' Market), but be aware that you'll have to sift through a fair amount of what can only be described as junk to find it. Bring small notes, as the prices are almost astonishingly low, and change is a perennial problem. Just don't give into the temptation of buying tiles at the Feira da Ladra, as most have been illegally ripped off buildings. If you feel an overwhelming urge to take home a Portuguese tile or two, head to an authorised dealer, such as d'Orey Azulejos, on Rua do Alecrim, where the wares are legitimately sourced.

05 Historic
LISBON

IMPRESSIVE | FRAUGHT | OMNIPRESENT

▬▬▬ Lisbon is Europe's second-oldest city, after Athens, so history is pretty much everywhere you look. There are the remains of a Roman amphitheatre dating from 57 CE and numerous gorgeous old churches, as well as the setting-off point for many of the maritime explorations that would see the Portuguese flag planted across three continents. There are even the remnants of a 20-million-year-old coral reef!

MILOSK50/SHUTTERSTOCK ©

📷 How to

Getting here Belém is quite a hike from central Lisbon, so kill two birds with one stone and experience one of Lisbon's famed trams by taking the 15E line.

When to go During the summer tourist high season, queues at historic sites can be daunting; visit during spring or autumn if possible.

Call ahead Visits to some sites, particularly those that are privately owned, must be booked in advance. It's generally best to call ahead to check.

STOCKPHOTOSART/SHUTTERSTOCK ©

LISBON EXPERIENCES

Left Torre de Belém **Far left top** Igreja de São Domingos **Far left bottom** Sala do Despacho, Palácio Nacional da Ajuda

The earthquake of 1755 No single event marked both the geography and psychology of the city as deeply as the devastating 1755 earthquake, which was followed by a tidal wave, as well as deadly fires. Memory of the traumatic triple-whammy catastrophe, which flattened much of the old city, remains deeply imprinted on the collective consciousness. To get a sense of the devastation it wrought, check out the **Convento do Carmo**, the ruins of a Gothic monastery that was destroyed in the quake.

Another of the sites lost in the earthquake was the Paço da Ribeira, the extravagant royal palace that was built in what is now the Praça do Comércio during the Age of Discovery and was said to contain incalculable treasures. Still, its replacement, the **Palácio Nacional da Ajuda** – in the western Ajuda neighbourhood to which the royal family decamped after the disaster – is open to the public and well worth the visit.

The Age of Discovery The hub of Age of Discovery sites is **Belém**, the western Lisbon neighbourhood along the Tagus from where many maritime expeditions set sail. Two of the main symbols of the period, the **Torre de Belém**, a four-storey-tall river fortification, and the nearby **Mosteiro dos Jerónimos**, a Gothic monastery that was begun shortly after Vasco de Gama's historic 1498 voyage to India, came through the 1755 quake remarkably unscathed.

🏛 The Churches of Lisbon

With some 120 churches – many of them built during the heyday of Portuguese wealth and power – there are plenty of breathtaking options to choose from. Here are a few standouts:

Igreja de São Domingos This marred beauty in the Santa Maria Maior neighbourhood has known tragedy in the form of floods, earthquakes and, finally, a devastating 1959 fire that makes it unlike any other church you've ever seen.

Igreja de São Roque This Baroque masterpiece survived the 1755 earthquake with hardly a scratch and is indisputably one of the most jaw-dropping churches in the city.

A Proud but Fraught History

THE FEATS OF EXPLORERS HAVE COME UNDER SCRUTINY

The Portuguese take great pride in the feats of their forebears, the intrepid navigators who, starting in the early 15th century, set sail for parts unknown, eventually claiming vast swaths of land stretching from South America all the way to East Asia.

BRADLEYSMITH/SHUTTERSTOCK ©

A Globe-Spanning Empire

Centuries before the British, the Portuguese had already built an empire upon which the sun never set: after claiming Ceuta, the now-Spanish enclave in present-day Morocco, in 1415, a series of Portuguese navigators spent much of the first half of the 15th century working their way down the western coast of Africa, in search of new trade routes and 'discovering' a series of islands, including Madeira and Cape Verde, along the way. Vasco de Gama reached India's western coast just years ahead of Pedro Álvarez Cabral's 1500 arrival in Brazil. Portugal's Diogo Ziemoto is said to be one of the two first Europeans to alight in Japan, in 1542.

'The Portuguese started something that radically changed the history of the world,' said historian João Paulo Oliveira e Costa, a professor at the Universidade Nova de Lisboa and the author of more than a dozen books on the Portuguese expansion. 'The Age of Discovery was, by any measure, indisputably positive for humanity.'

Portugal's Role in Enslavement

But a growing cadre of academics, journalists, artists and activists are questioning the supposed gloriousness of the Age of Discovery and are reexamining the role Portugal's empire played in the enslavement of millions of Africans.

Portugal pioneered the Atlantic trade of enslaved people, which began in 1444, with the sale in the southern Portuguese city of Lagos of more than 200 people seized from the then-recently discovered coast of West Africa.

Left Padrão dos Descobrimentos (Monument to the Discoveries) **Middle** Vasco de Gama **Right** Mappa mundi fragment, Padrão dos Descobrimentos

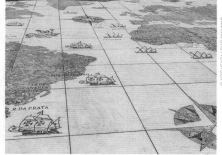

Over the next 400 years, Portuguese vessels are believed to have transported an estimated 5.8 million enslaved Africans. By contrast, Portugal's nearest rival in the trade of enslaved people, the British, are estimated to have transported some 3.2 million enslaved Africans.

A growing cadre of academics, journalists, artists and activists are questioning the supposed gloriousness of the Age of Discovery.

Memorialising the Past

While the vast majority of enslaved Africans sold by the Portuguese ended up in the country's mammoth South American colony, Brazil, the practice of owning enslaved people was also widespread in Portugal itself. It is estimated that as early as the 16th century, one out of 10 Lisbon residents was an enslaved African. And yet Lisbon has never had a monument honouring enslaved peoples' historic contribution to the city, nor one marking Portugal's commanding role in the Atlantic trade of enslaved people.

But that's about to change. In 2017, city residents approved a project to build a memorial to enslaved people. Imagined by Angolan artist Kiluanji Kia Henda, the memorial will turn Lisbon's central Campo das Cebolas into a sugarcane plantation, made up of 560 sugarcane stalks in black aluminum – in a nod to the 'white gold' that helped fuel the Atlantic trade of enslaved people. The memorial will constitute Portugal's most significant mea culpa to date for its role in the trade of enslaved people.

ⓘ The Myth of the 'Bons Colonizadores'

'The myth that the Portuguese colonial expansion was something benign, the "first globalisation", is everywhere in Portugal – spread not only in our schools, but also on TV, in advertising, in the monuments that dot our cities. It's crucial we dismantle those myths,' said Beatriz Gomes Dias, a lawmaker who is among the three Black women currently serving in the Portuguese parliament. 'Even through we of course cannot change what happened in the past, we can change the way we speak about that history today. And that will change the way we act in the present.'

Beatriz Gomes Dias,
Assembly of the Public of Portugal

06 Hidden GEMS

GARDENS | MARKETS | MUSEUMS

▬▬▬ While it may feel like a village, Lisbon is a city of 2.8 million inhabitants – with the vast majority of the metropolis generally off the beaten path. But venture even further afield and you can find the hidden treasures that make this city truly unique.

🗺 How to

Getting around Use the metro to get to more distant points of interest. Clean, cheap and efficient, Lisbon's metro works best for covering longer distances.

When to go While Lisbon has plenty of must-sees, devote one day out of a week-long visit to checking out spots off the beaten track.

COVID-19 closures The pandemic has hit Portugal hard, and it's not clear what will ultimately survive. Check before heading out.

Lisbon's discretion and laid-back attitude extends to many of its most interesting spots. Sure, there are are a few downright remarkable places – including the Tile Museum and the Oceanário aquarium, as well as the rickety but iconic Number 28 tramline – that get all the attention, but there are also a slew of really interesting sites that fly under the radar, not only of most visitors but even of many residents.

Museu do Traje One such place is the Museu Nacional do Traje (Costume Museum), which traces the evolution of Portuguese fashion from the 17th century to the present day. Located in a former aristocratic mansion in the northern neighbourhood of Lumiar, the museum is a fun visit even for those who couldn't care about clothing thanks to its sumptuous, sculpture-studded grounds and quirky restaurant. It's a wonderful spot for

🛍 Shop Like a Local

Skip the supermarket and have an authentic Portuguese market experience at the **Mercado de Arroios**, a produce market in the working-class neighbourhood of Arroios. And be sure to check out **Mezze**, a mouth-watering Middle Eastern restaurant run by a nonprofit that helps refugees.

Left Reservatório da Mãe d'Água das Amoreiras (p73) **Above left** Jardim Botânico Tropical de Lisboa (p72) **Above right** Metro station, Lisbon

an afternoon pick-me-up and leisurely stroll through the garden for both clothes horses and the fashion averse alike.

Jardim Botânico Tropical de Lisboa Not to be confused with any of the city's multiple other botanical gardens, the Jardim Botânico Tropical de Lisboa is a lush enclave in Belém that's so rife with tropical flora brought back from Portugal's former colonies it's said to have its own microclimate. But it also has a dark past: in 1940, under the regime of dictator António Salazar, it was the site of a human zoo, with the Portuguese public lining up to gawk at whole families snatched from their homes in Guinea-Bissau and other Portuguese territories in Africa. This is clearly not something the management is interested in highlighting – the information pamphlet makes no mention of the shameful incident – and the busts of African men and women that dot the grounds are the only hints of that little-known history.

🛳 Ferry Back in Time to Trafaria

Just a 20-minute ferry ride away from Belém, Trafaria feels mind-blowingly distant, both geographically and temporally. A stroll around the town, with its motley fleet of wooden boats and picturesque collection of weather-beaten buildings, plunges visitors back into Portugal's not-so-distant past, when much of the population lived as they had centuries earlier. What Trafaria lacks in must-visit sites it makes up for in vivid character. Plus, if you rent a bike from a stand near the ferry terminal in Belém, you can cycle from Trafaria to São João de Caparica, and from there down the coast.

Left Ferry disembarkation, Trafaria
Below Sculpture, Jardim Botânico
Tropical de Lisboa

Reservatório da Mãe d'Água das Amoreiras

A site whose name literally translates as 'the mother of waters' might sound like a strange place to visit, and indeed this 18th-century water reservoir might initially seem like a quirky choice. But with its gorgeous arched ceilings, placid pools and verdant fountains, this landmark on the equally beautiful Praça das Amoreiras, where the city's silk weavers were once concentrated, is not only a key part of Lisbon's history, but also just a beautiful spot to take in something weird and wonderful.

Igreja do Convento dos Cardaes You could probably walk by the plain facade of the Cardaes Convent hundreds of times without suspecting that behind the walls lies an opulent, gold- and tile-drenched gem. Built in the 17th century, and showcasing not only the sheer wealth but also the actual gold that was extracted from Brazil, this convent survived the 1755 quake largely unscathed.

By Jenny Barchfield
Jenny is a multilingual journalist, media professional and consultant, happily based in Lisbon, Portugal.

LISBON ESSAY

Captivated by Lisbon

EMIGRATION TO LISBON BRINGS A LIGHTNESS OF SPIRIT

As a longtime foreign correspondent, I'm no stranger to moving. I've lived in half-a-dozen countries on three continents. I was in Paris the longest – more than a decade – and after I left, spent the subsequent decade pining for the City of Light, until... Lisbon.

When I moved to Lisbon, it was almost by default. I was living in Rio de Janeiro at the time and feeling generally unmoored after my wrenching move away from Paris. I wanted to buy a place in order to feel anchored somewhere – anywhere, really – in the world. My first choice was, naturally, Paris. But, alas, on my journalist's salary, that was all but impossible.

One day I was chatting with a Parisian friend who had just returned from a magical weekend in Lisbon. She mentioned how affordable real estate in the city was, and that offhand comment got me thinking: I have an EU passport and speak Portuguese. So why not buy a place in Lisbon?

It was a crazy plan on the face of it. After all, I had spent only a few days in Portugal as a teenager, decades earlier. But my enthusiasm went a long way towards making up for my ignorance, and after months spent trolling online real-estate sites, I touched down in Lisbon for what I had come to think of as a two-week-long 'mission': I was bound and determined to buy an apartment. As luck would have it, I managed it, signing on a gem of a place – two bedrooms right next to a glorious park.

I had finally secured a place in the world – albeit one that I had no intention of actually moving into. In fact, because of my job as a correspondent with a news agency, I couldn't have moved in even if I had wanted to. But just knowing that I finally had some 70 sq metres to call my own brought a measure of peace to my nomad's heart.

A few years later, though, my professional circumstances changed, and I decided to retreat to my Lisbon apartment. Even as I prepared my Portugal-bound shipment, I was nearly as clueless about my new homeland as I had been

Left Ponte 25 de Abril at sunset **Middle** New homeowner Jenny Barchfield **Right** Palácio dos Marqueses de Fronteira

when I set out on my laser-focused mission. Truth be told, even as I boarded the flight to Lisbon, I still wished that I were moving back to Paris.

It wouldn't take long, however, for that to change. Lisbon, I soon discovered, has a remarkable lightness about it – lightness in every sense of the word. Firstly and most literally, the city is bathed in a luminosity I have yet to experience almost anywhere else in Europe: golden sunlight not only illuminates the sky, but it bounces off the Tagus and off the little limestone cubes that make up the hallmark sidewalks, making the city almost glow.

> I touched down in Lisbon for what I had come to think of as a two-week-long 'mission'.

But I also mean lightness in the sense of levity – of ease and calm and buoyancy. At a time when the market plays such an outsized role in setting the tone of our societies and even our own individual lives, Portugal, with its fewer than 11 million inhabitants, is simply too small to matter much. This means that the forces that have ratcheted up the pace and pressure in many other global metropolises are largely absent from Lisbon. The stakes here are just lower – in the best possible way. And then there are the people: the Portuguese are warm and welcoming and modest and funny and curious, and friends came more easily here than in other places I've lived.

The more time I've spent in Lisbon, moving leisurely through this luminous city, surrounded by a close-knit and loving group of friends, the surer I am that, thanks to an accident of real estate, I have finally found my place in the world.

⚗ A Avó Veio Trabalhar

Both the name of a little charity shop selling an array of homewares and handmade clothes and the social project that's behind it, A Avó Veio Trabalhar literally translates as 'the grandma who came to work'. And work she does! Since its founding in 2014, the initiative has been combating social isolation by drawing retired people out of their homes and bringing them together with people of all ages to collaborate on creative projects. Everything for sale in the shop, including cute throw pillows and vibrant, artful blankets, is handmade using the techniques that many of the retirees learned as children.

Listings

BEST OF THE REST

🍴 Local Faves & Far-Flung Flavours

Clube dos Jornalistas €€€

Housed in the sumptuous townhouse that was formerly Lisbon's Journalists' Club, this relaxed but refined restaurant in Estrela serves up Portuguese food with a twist.

Plano Restaurante €€€

A favourite of 100 Maneiras chef Ljubomir Stanisic, this intimate Portuguese restaurant in Graça serves up a nine-course tasting menu in a stunning outdoor setting.

Prado €€€

Another Stanisic favourite, this high-end restaurant by talented young chef António Galapito is seasonally driven and emphasises locally sourced ingredients.

Essencial €€€

For refined, French-inspired food in a chic minimalist setting, try this small Bairro Alto restaurant.

Taberna da Rua das Flores €€

Another, more affordable, option for those seeking traditional Portuguese food with a contemporary twist (at least for those armed with enough patience to brave the often-intimidating queue).

O Frade €€

A stone's throw from the historic sites in Belém, this restaurant specialises in food from the Alentejo region – just the hardy fuel you need to power through a day of sightseeing.

Água Pela Barba €€

Standout dishes at this inventive seafood spot in Bica include the saffron risotto with prawns, fish tacos and octopus.

Tentações de Goa €€

Sample revelatory Indian fare at this hole-in-the-wall joint near Martim Moniz that specialises in food from Portugal's erstwhile foothold in India, the western coastal region of Goa.

A Cevicheria €€

With its giant octopus sculpture suspended from the ceiling, you can't miss this Peruvian restaurant, which has become one of the hottest spots in Príncipe Real.

Último Porto €€

This modest seafood restaurant on the Doca de Alcântara boasts solid food at reasonable prices and great views out onto the Tagus that have made it a Lisbon institution.

Clube Naval €€

Another riverside seafood joint, this one in Belém, boasting solid food and service and luminous views out over the river.

Arkhe €€

Inventive and artfully presented, this establishment just off of the Rua da Boavista takes vegetarian restaurants to new heights.

Landeau Chocolate

Quintal d'Santo Amaro €

The brainchild of a transplant from Rio de Janeiro, this tiny restaurant in Estrela serves up vegan variations on Brazilian classics like *feijoada*.

Mercearia da Mila €€

Founded in 2017 by a Portuguese man who returned from London with his English wife, this combined greengrocer-delicatessen-cafe, opposite the French Consulate in Santos, is a great spot for a coffee or a quick sandwich.

Pois Café €

Duck into this bohemian space in Alfama to lounge on one of the mismatched couches as you sip your coffee, slurp your fresh juice or nibble on a snack.

Café Belga €€

With so many great Portuguese wines, beers sometimes get short shrift in Lisbon. But not at this cosy cafe-bar in Graça, which has an enviable selection of Belgian beers on tap.

Gelato Davvero €

Ice cream is, of course, a subjective thing, but this shop in Santos serves up what is widely regarded as just about the best Italian gelato in Lisbon.

Landeau Chocolate €

This local chain, with several locations across Lisbon, has but one dessert on offer, a celebrated chocolate concoction that's equal parts *fondant au chocolat* and dark chocolate mousse.

Ti-Natércia €

Strictly in Portuguese, 'Aunt' Natércia serves up her downright delicious Portuguese home cooking with a side of superb storytelling in a teeny space deep in the heart of Alfama. Vegetarians may prefer to look elsewhere; definitely cash only.

Castelo de São Jorge

Architecture, Greenery & Art

Castelo de São Jorge

With sections that date back to the 6th century, this fortress has seen successive waves of conquerers, including the Romans and the Visigoths, and boasts privileged views out over the city.

Casa dos Bicos

This unique 16th-century townhouse near the Terreiro do Paço is a museum honouring the late great Portuguese writer José Saramago, winner of the 1998 Nobel Prize in Literature.

Estufa Fria

This charming greenhouse complex in the Parque Eduardo VII houses botanical gardens filled with flora from different climates.

Fundação das Casas Fronteira e Alorna

Book in advance to take a guided tour of the lavish, tile-covered palace (and manicured grounds) that are still in the hands of the aristocratic family that built it in the 17th century.

Escola Portuguesa de Arte Equestre

Portugal's answer to the Spanish Riding School in Vienna, this is an essential visit for horse lovers. In addition to watching their formal performances, you can reserve to attend one of their daily training sessions.

Cinema Ideal

This little arthouse movie theatre in Chiado boasts the best the city's best cinematic lineup. (Note that the subtitles are in Portuguese!)

Fundação Calouste Gulbenkian

Nestled within the grounds of a verdant park, this art museum holds one of the world's largest private art collections, which was assembled by Armenian-born oil baron Calouste Gulbenkian.

Casa-Museu Medeiros e Almeida

Once the mansion of another gentleman entrepreneur and art collector, this museum off Avenida Liberdade is packed with priceless treasures from the world over.

Museu Coleção Berardo

Culture fiends can get their contemporary-art fix at Museu Coleção Berardo, where the ultrawhite, minimalist gallery displays billionaire José Berardo's eye-popping collection of abstract, surrealist and pop art.

🍷 Distinctive Drinking & Dancing

Damas €

Popular with students, this restaurant-bar in Graça is also a live-music venue, showcasing a wide variety of different acts.

Bairro Alto Hotel Rooftop Bar €€€

On the opposite end of the spectrum from Damas, the rooftop bar of the newly refurbished Bairro Alto Hotel in Chiado boasts amazing views out over the Praça Camões.

Tabernáculo by Hernâni Miguel €€

Born in Guinea-Bissau and raised in Portugal, the namesake and owner of this wine bar and gastropub in Cais do Sodré brings together African-inspired foods, Portuguese wines and Brazilian music.

Alfaiataria Bar €€

Just a few doors down the Rua de São Paulo from Tabernáculo, this LGBTIQ-focused bar welcomes everyone with its warm and friendly vibes.

Memmo Alfama €€

Alfama unfolds like origami from the stylishly decked roof terrace of the Memmo Alfama hotel. Stop by for the dreamy vistas over the rooftops, spires and Rio Tejo and stay for a sundowner.

Majong €€

This bohemian cocktail bar in Bairro Alto serves up personalised drinks based on customers' preferences.

🛍 Antiques, Handicrafts & Gifts

Brisa Galeria

Founded in 2018 by an enchanting couple from Rio de Janeiro, this space in Chiado has emerged as one of Lisbon's most interesting galleries.

Companhia Portugueza dos Chás

Tea lovers mustn't miss this tea and tea-accoutrement store housed in a former shoe shop dating from 1880 that brings together an aromatic selection of loose leaf teas sourced from around the world.

Cinema Ideal

Rua de São Bento

For a dizzying selection of antiques spanning centuries, head to this street in Estrela, where shop after shop is packed with truly unique wares.

Tania Gil jewelry – wearable objects

A veritable treasure trove of unique gifts, this little shop in Santos showcases the work of talented young jeweller Tania Gil.

Chapelaria Azevedo Rua

This historic hat shop off the Praça Dom Pedro IV also custom makes a wide variety of high-quality headgear for surprisingly affordable prices.

Filipe Faísca

Among Portugal's top designers, Faísca does inventive contemporary takes on traditional Portuguese garb, like oversized cocoon coats made out of shepherds' blankets and fetching button-down shirts with handmade lace cutouts.

ICON Shop

The top contemporary designers and makers of all sorts of objects, from ceramics and leather goods to jewellery and textiles, are represented at this store in Chiado.

Restrosaria Rosa Pomar

This knitting supply shop in Bairro Alto is *the* place to go for quality Portuguese yarns.

Embaixada

d'Orey Azulejos

If you feel an overwhelming urge to take home a Portuguese tile or two, prevent the defacing of historic buildings by heading to this authorised dealer, where the wares are legitimately sourced.

Embaixada

Housed in an exquisite 19th-century neo-Moorish palace, this unique shopping centre has boutiques selling everything from vintage records to organic cosmetics, eco-homewares, contemporary Portuguese ceramics and catwalk styles.

Flores Textile Studio

Another top destination for Portuguese-made homewares, this store on the Praça das Flores offers up an extensive range of pillows, rugs and blankets.

Scan to find more things to do in Lisbon online

BEYOND
LISBON

NATURE | HISTORY | CULTURE

Dive and explore the marine life of the **Berlengas Archipelago** (p98)
🕑 1 day

Fátima (Cova da Iria)●

Parque Natural das Serras de Aire e Candeeiros

Caldas da Rainha●

Óbidos●

Indulge yourself in reading at **Óbidos'** bookstores (p96)
🕑 1 day

Rio Tejo

Torres Vedras ●

E S T R E M A D U R A

Parque Natural de Sintra-Cascais

Go up to **Palácio Nacional da Pena** for an incredible view of the Serra de Sintra (p85)
🕑 1 day

LISBON ✪

Cascais
Almada●
●**Montijo**

Atlantic Ocean

Enjoy SUP or kayak in the **Parque Natural da Serra da Arrábida** (p91)
🕑 ½ day

Setúbal Península

●**Setúbal**

●Alcácer do Sal

Rio Sado

BEYOND LISBON
Trip Builder

▬▬ Let your imagination run free with tales from another time, or allow yourself to be conquered by natural parks and animal sanctuaries. Beyond Lisbon, there is a region that leaves no one indifferent, especially lovers of good food and fabulous wines.

Sines
●

Take a boat trip along the **Rio Sado** to spot dolphins (p90)
🕑 ½ day

B A I X O
A L E N T E J O

Parque Natural do Sudoeste Alentejano e Costa Vicentina

Ⓝ 0 ———————— 50 km
　 0 ———————— 25 miles

Practicalities

ARRIVING

Estação Ferroviária de Sete Rios, in Lisbon, is where the train leaves to Setúbal.

Estação Rodoviária do Campo Grande, also in Lisbon, has buses to Peniche and Óbidos.

FIND YOUR WAY

Look for the Posto de Turismo, which has information about what to see and do.

MONEY

Carry some cash just in case, but credit cards are accepted almost everywhere, and there are numerous ATMs.

WHERE TO STAY

Location	Atmosphere
Sintra	Old chalets, century-old manor houses, or small apartments near the monuments.
Setúbal	Cheaper options in the city centre; book in advance.
Óbidos	Charming properties in the medieval town for a complete experience.
Berlengas	Book a surf house in Peniche, just a boat ride from the islands.

EATING & DRINKING

Sangria A great option if you enjoy sweeter drinks. Red, white or with sparkling wine, almost all restaurants serve it. Just make sure it is freshly made.

Must-try clams
Caught in Lagoa de Óbidos; ask for them cooked *à bulhão pato*, in olive oil, garlic and coriander (p103)

Best fish
Setúbal or Peniche. With large fishing ports, it is as fresh as you can get (p103)

GETTING AROUND

Driving is the best way to visit the cities around Lisbon. There is a vast network of highways that makes it easier and faster to get around.

Buses are a great option to get to the towns further away from the capital. Rodoviária do Oeste serves cities like Peniche, Nazaré and Óbidos and depart from Campo Grande.

JAN–MAR	APR–JUN	JUL–SEP	OCT–DEC
Rainy season, ideal for visiting museums and monuments	Mild temperatures, perfect for outdoor activities	Hot and dry weather; the busiest time of the year	Temperatures drop; calls for local comfort food

Unknown
SINTRA

MONUMENTS | WALKING | NATURE

▬▬▬ Sintra was the first place in Europe to be listed by Unesco as a Cultural Landscape, and it is this very landscape that attracts visitors from all over the world. Sintra is full of lavish palaces, manors and villas, not to mention its imposing castle. But among the lush scenery of this Portuguese town are secrets worth unraveling.

STEFANO_VALERI/SHUTTERSTOCK ©

🗺 **How to**

Getting here Take the train at Estação do Rossio, in Lisbon. From Sintra station, several buses go to the main monuments. Avoid taking a car into Sintra's historical centre, as several streets have limited access.

When to go Weekdays and low season are your best option. During the summer months and at weekends, the town fills up with visitors.

Hiking There are several trails that cross the natural park and lead to the main monuments of Sintra.

SAIKO3P/SHUTTERSTOCK ©

AGSAZ/SHUTTERSTOCK ©

BEYOND LISBON EXPERIENCES

Left Dining room, Palácio Nacional da Pena **Far left top** Palácio de Monserrate **Far left bottom** Castelo dos Mouros

Palace tours Sintra's palaces are a must for everyone who visits what is considered the most romantic village in Portugal. But what if you could see them exclusively, just you and your travel companions? Sintra's **Palácio Nacional da Pena**, the **Palácio Nacional de Queluz** and the **Palácio de Monserrate** open their doors after hours for those who want to visit them on a private tour, accompanied by experts who know every corner of these historic buildings.

Going backstage There is more to Sintra than meets the eye. Places that are usually closed to the public are now accessible in the company of specialists in the most diverse areas.

Access the interior of the great dome of the yellow tower of **Palácio Nacional da Pena** to see works of art and objects that have never been on display, and climb the clock tower to have one of the best views of this World Heritage site.

Learn about the past and the people who passed through Sintra on a visit to the **Castelo dos Mouros**, guided by the archaeologist responsible for recent excavations.

Follow the tunnels that form the network of water mines that cross the mountain's interior in the company of a historian, or walk through the **Tapada de Monserrate** guided by a biologist who explains all the work done to preserve the local ecosystem.

✅ Accessible Sintra

As one of the most visited locations in the Lisbon region, Sintra's monuments have adapted to visitors with special needs.

Under the project 'Parques de Sintra Welcome Better', accessibility improvements include the introduction of ramps and lift platforms, the capacity for wheelchairs in tourist buses, and even the introduction of electric wheelchairs for nature walks, among other things.

Visitors with special needs can also count on tours with an interpreter of Portuguese Sign Language and International Sign Language, as well as sensorial experiences.

SINTRA'S
Architectural Treasures

01 Palácio Nacional da Pena

The most emblematic monument in Sintra; an outstanding example of 19th-century Portuguese Romanticism.

02 Quinta da Regaleira

One of the most enigmatic places in Sintra. The architecture and landscape have the signature of Luigi Manini, emphasising the Neo-Manueline and Renaissance styles.

03 Palácio Nacional de Sintra

For almost eight centuries, this palace served as a residence for the Portuguese monarchy and court.

04 Palácio Nacional de Queluz

Constructed in the 18th century as a summer palace, it was home to two generations of monarchs. It stands out for its opulent rooms and lush gardens.

05 Castelo dos Mouros

Built between the 8th and 9th centuries, this is a remarkable Islamic testament in the region. The top of the castle offers one of the best views over Sintra.

06 Convento dos Capuchos

Also known as the 'Cork Convent'. With simple features, it is surrounded by dense vegetation.

07 Villa Sassetti

The construction takes inspiration from the Lombard castles that originated in Northern Italy.

08 Palácio de Monserrate

With exotic and vegetal motifs, the interior decoration of this palace blends in with the natural park that surrounds it.

09 Chalet da Condessa d'Elba

Built in the 19th century, following the model of alpine chalets. The chalet's garden has botanical varieties from all over the world.

MATIAS PLANAS/SHUTTERSTOCK ©

Mystic Sintra

DISCOVER A PLACE SURROUNDED BY MYTHS AND LEGENDS

If you think that Sintra is one of the most beautiful and exciting places in the Lisbon area, wait until you get to know all the myths and legends that characterise this enchanting town.

'Magical things happen every day here.' Jorge Vassalo has no doubt that Sintra is one of the most extraordinary places in the world. The Portuguese travel writer, who has toured countless countries and is lucky enough to call Sintra home, recognises the mysticism surrounding the architecture and history of this place.

'Starting with the fog and the microclimate, which lend it a mysterious aura. And it is no coincidence that, since time immemorial, the so-called "Moon's Mount" has influenced and inspired so many different people – from poets to royalty, tourists, and other artists. From Palácio da Pena to Cabo da Roca, there is a concentration of energy here that is unique in the world – that no matter how much I travel, I can hardly reproduce anywhere else,' he says.

The myths and legends surrounding Sintra have existed for hundreds of years, passed down from generation to generation, clinging to the inhabitants who passed through and those who still live there.

Each place tells its own story, and many involve heartbreaks, ghosts, and mysterious and magical beings.

Legends that Stand the Test of Time

One of the most popular places is Quinta da Regaleira. In this property designed by Italian architect Luigi Manini, there is no shortage of references to Masonic and Templar symbols. One of the great attractions of this estate is the well of Quinta de Regaleira, 'where a ritual of descent to the nine hells used to take place, followed by a dark passage through caves that lead to waterfalls that represent the Garden of Eden,' says Vassalo.

Left Convento dos Capuchos **Middle** Quinta da Regaleira **Right** Palácio de Seteais

The name of the Palácio de Seteais is also related to the story of a Moorish princess who would die if she said *'ai'* seven times and ended up doing so as a result of a broken heart.

But other stories are spread throughout time and space in Sintra. Such as the Legend of the Tomb of the Two Brothers, which tells the story of the siblings who fought to the death for the love of a Moorish girl; the Legend of Friar Honório, an inhabitant of the Convento dos Capuchos, who crossed paths with the Devil in female form; or the Legend of the Fairy Cave, which says that every night a fairy appears near a grotto at the entrance of Parque da Pena.

> The myths and legends surrounding Sintra have existed for hundreds of years, passed down from generation to generation.

The magic of Sintra seems to be far from over. 'There is a snowball effect, in which the consequences of some are the causes of others. In other words: the more artists write, paint and fall in love with the mystique of Sintra, the more that mystique grows. It is, without a doubt, a unique place. Here you feel that naive, almost childlike fascination for mystery and adventure. It's really a fairy tale,' confirms the Portuguese writer, for whom it is difficult to choose the most mystical place in his homeland: 'between the gardens of the Palácio de Monserrate and the Convento dos Capuchos, the Azenhas do Mar and Praia da Ursa, for example... I don't even know which one evokes more memories for me. But there is a small garden in São Pedro de Sintra, overlooking the Palácio da Pena and the Castelo dos Mouros...which, at sunset, has a unique mystique.'

Specialising in Myths & Legends

The Posto de Turismo de Sintra is now an interpretive centre that reveals all the myths and legends around this town.

The museum features 17 immersive spaces, spread over four floors, that use scenography, multimedia and sensory experiences to tell legendary stories.

Inaugurated in 2015, Sintra Myths and Legends relied on the work of a large team of architects, set designers, scriptwriters, historians and experts in audiovisuals and 3D and augmented reality techniques to create a fun and captivating experience for all visitors.

08 Explore
SETÚBAL

NATURAL PARK | WINE | BEACHES

Setúbal is one of Portugal's main ports, and with that comes a more industrial feel. But this is also the city of the best fried cuttlefish in the country, and where a simple boat trip to the Tróia Peninsula can bring dolphins along the way. Then there's the crystal-clear beaches of the Serra da Arrábida, and the famous regional wines.

BENOIT BACOU/GETTY IMAGES ©

🗺 How to

Getting here Take the train to Setúbal, which leaves from the Roma/ Areeiro station in Lisbon, and takes about an hour to get here. By car via the highway is faster.

When to go The best time is mid-season, avoiding the weekends.

In the warm months the area's beaches fill up, and roads become heavily congested.

Observation Take a boat trip to see the bottlenose dolphins that live in the Rio Sado estuary.

ALEXANDRE ROTENBERG/SHUTTERSTOCK ©

ALEXANDRE ROTENBERG/SHUTTERSTOCK ©

BEYOND LISBON EXPERIENCES

Left Vineyard, Setúbal **Far left top** Praia Galapinhos **Far left bottom** José Maria da Fonseca winery, Azeitão

Ocean inspired The calm and transparent sea, nestled in a small cove of fine sand, has earned **Praia Galapinhos** international recognition and made it an unmissable site in the **Parque Natural da Serra da Arrábida**. But other small stretches of sand lie just a short distance away, waiting to be discovered.

Let the ocean continue to dictate your tour and accept the challenge of a stand-up paddleboarding session at **Portinho da Arrábida** or a diving experience at **Parque Marinho Luiz Saldanha**. This protected marine area stretches from the exit of the Sado estuary to the north of Cabo Espichel.

From the city to the mountain There are several museums in Setúbal that provide insight into the city's history. The **Museu do Trabalho Michel Giacometti** is one such space, showing the town's connection to fishing and the old canneries and lithographies. Head to the interior of Serra da Arrábida to visit an ancient convent of Franciscan monks (only by appointment) and make a stop at **Forte Santa Maria**, which houses an oceanographic museum.

Local wine It is impossible to go to Setúbal and not taste the wine produced in one of Portugal's leading winemaking regions. Don't leave without trying the famous Moscatel de Setúbal, a wine with a sweet and fruity flavour.

🍇 Best Setúbal Peninsula Wineries

José Maria da Fonseca One of the oldest wineries in the area, where the big old wooden barrels rest in long aisles to the sound of Gregorian chants. Here you can taste the historic fortified wine of this region: Moscatel.

Quinta de Alcube An incredible winery with Roman remains, including the old baths and an underground aqueduct. And yes, you can taste good white and red wines here, along with Azeitão cheese or an egg tart.

Recommended by **Madalena Vidigal**, *wine tourism expert and author of entrevinhas.com*

09 When in ÓBIDOS

HISTORY | CASTLE | BOOKS

Some choose to dress up in traditional medieval costumes, and others prefer to stop at every little shop to see the craftwork or taste a glass of Ginginha. Óbidos is the most famous medieval village in Portugal, and its streets hide centuries of history and activities to discover. From monuments to books, you can spend several days here without ever getting bored.

🗺 How to

Getting here Car is the best option to get to Óbidos. The trip takes one hour from Lisbon. There is a paid parking lot at the entrance of the village.

When to go Choose weekdays to explore Óbidos, as the village is flooded with visitors on weekends.

Drink Learn about the history of Ginginha de Óbidos and surrender to the sweet taste of this decadent liqueur made from sour cherries.

Left Street performers, Óbidos **Far left top** Castelo de Óbidos **Far left bottom** Ginginha de Óbidos stall

Hands-on The Óbidos handicraft known as Verguinha de Óbidos is one of the town's attractions. At **Oficina do Barro** you can enrol in a workshop to learn the history of these ceramic pieces and how they are produced. In the end, you get to take your *verguinha* home!

If you are a music fan, at the **Luthier Workshop** you can discover how a musical instrument is built, examine the tools and materials used in the process, and see projects in various stages of completion.

Escape the tower Enter one of the **Castelo de Óbidos** towers to play a hands-on escape game. Here you will be invited to solve mysteries related to facts and curiosities about the village of Óbidos.

Óbidos flavours Besides the Ginginha de Óbidos, there are other flavours to discover in this medieval town. Try the traditional cake called Ferradura, or delight yourself with the local chorizos accompanied by freshly baked bread. Picnic on the castle walls overlooking one of the best views in town. But don't stop there: end the day with an experience of wine and tapas on the terrace of **Casa do Arco**.

☆ Festivals in Óbidos

Festival Internacional de Chocolate Held since 2002, between April and May, this festival is dedicated to chocolate lovers. From sculptures to workshops, show cooking and competitions, everything is devoted to this sweet ingredient.

Óbidos Medieval Market Between July and August the town fills up with jugglers, tavern keepers, knights and maidens, among numereous other medieval characters. There are also tournaments, music and theatre performances.

Óbidos Christmas Village During December, Christmas magic invades Óbidos. Count on numerous activities and shows and don't miss the traditional Christmas market and, of course, Santa Claus.

ÓBIDOS'
Medieval Heritage

01 Capela de São Martinho

Founded in 1331, it is the only religious temple in Óbidos that maintains its medieval appearance.

02 Porta da Vila

An oratory of Nossa Senhora da Piedade, patron saint of Óbidos. It's located on a baroque balcony at the main entrance to the village.

03 Praça de Santa Maria

Built between the 14th and 15th centuries, following a Renaissance layout.

04 Rua Direita

The route that connects the village entrance to the Paço dos Alcaides. It gained its name in the 14th century.

05 Igreja de São Pedro

The church still has traces of an old Gothic portal and has a baroque altarpiece from the Joanine period inside.

06 Igreja de São Tiago

Constructed in 1186, it served the Alcaides and the military garrison, and was the Portuguese queens' and court chapel.

07 Castelo de Óbidos and Paço dos Alcaides

The town's most emblematic monument and its palace underwent several expansions between the 13th and 16th centuries.

08 Igreja de São João Baptista

Built by Queen Saint Elizabeth's order to serve as a leper hospital in the late 13th and early 14th centuries.

The Literary City

BOOKS BREATHE NEW LIFE INTO MEDIEVAL ÓBIDOS

In December 2015, the medieval town of Óbidos was awarded 'Literary City' status – a title granted by Unesco acknowledging the role that books have been playing in the regeneration and growth of the town.

The Igreja de Santiago appears high at the top of the stairs at the end of the busiest street in Óbidos. Right next to the castle walls, it was built in the 12th century to provide spiritual support to the military and nobility that passed through the medieval town.

Today, the scene inside that church is different. Yes, the altar is still there, but the aisle is now filled with shelves stocked with books.

The Santiago Church was the first major bookstore to open in the historic centre of Óbidos, the result of an ambitious initiative to celebrate the town's heritage.

The Óbidos Vila Literária (Literary Village) project emerged in 2011 from 'the need to rehabilitate some buildings and public spaces'. At the time, 'the national context was that of a country without funding programmes for the area of conservation and heritage, so it was necessary to find solutions that aimed at a cultural and economic dimension of the space and that simultaneously respected the history of the buildings. The strategy was to create a cultural and literary hub within Óbidos,' says Carla Pinho, project manager of Óbidos Unesco Creative City of Literature.

Igreja de Santiago was thus the first of a vast literary network installed in different spaces, public and private, extending throughout the municipality. In Óbidos' historical centre it includes places such as the Casa José Saramago, named after the Portuguese Literature Nobel Prize winner; the Livraria do Mercado Biológico, which occupies an old fire station and, as the name in Portuguese suggests, holds a small market of local products; and the Literary Man Hotel, accommodation outside the walls, totally dedicated to the theme of books.

Left Livraria de Santiago **Middle** Livraria do Mercado Biológico **Right** Book flea market, Óbidos

FAINA GUREVICH/SHUTTERSTOCK ©

'The different bookstores in the county are differentiated by the theme to which each one is dedicated, creating a unique diversity,' Carla Pinho highlights.

For Book Lovers

Today, the village hosts major international literary events that attract visitors from all over the country and even the world.

The Óbidos International Literature Festival, which began in 2015, and is normally held in October, is one of them. For 11 days the town is packed with exhibitions, concerts, master classes, book launches, literature courses, conferences, seminars, performances, authors' meetings and round tables, and film cycles, among many other activities. With Portuguese and international authors presenting their latest works or talking about their most passionate themes, the venues fill to the brim, and the town goes into a frenzy.

> Óbidos' bookstores open their doors every day and offer solace to all those who seek knowledge and fun in the pages of a book.

Another major annual event, held between April and May, is Latitudes, a meeting point for travel literature lovers that offers four days full of activities including book launches, exhibitions and workshops.

Apart from the major events, Óbidos' bookstores open their doors every day and, like the Igreja de Santiago, offer solace to all those who seek knowledge and fun in the pages of a book.

✅ International Recognition

In 2015 Unesco named Óbidos a Literary City, thus integrating the town in the Creative Cities Network. The nomination led to an even greater focus on literature and books as one of the main forms of local development.

Giving Óbidos an utterly different touristic draw, the Creative City title also opened doors to new international opportunities, which is reflected in the annual activities program. One example is the artistic residencies organised in collaboration with other cities, such as Granada, Spain.

10 Berlengas' Natural **TREASURES**

NATURE | DIVING | WALKING

A paradise for birds and all nature lovers, the Berlengas Archipelago leaves no visitor indifferent. From walks leading to an ancient fortress, to the impressive caves and the fascination of the underwater world, the Berlengas emerge as a natural paradise that you will not want to miss.

TATIANA POPOVA/SHUTTERSTOCK ©

🗺 How to

Getting here To get to Berlenga Grande, you must take a boat that leaves from the Peniche harbor (daily May to September). Once on the island, all routes are conquered on foot.

When to go The crossings to the island take place during the high-season months. Outside that time you will have to book a private boat. Choose days with less swell to avoid getting seasick.

Around the island Take a boat trip to see the caves or go sport fishing or diving.

MARIO LAVRADOR/SHUTTERSTOCK ©

INACIO PIRES/SHUTTERSTOCK ©

BEYOND LISBON EXPERIENCES

Left Praia do Carreiro do Mosteiro, Berlenga Grande **Far left top** Forte São João Baptista **Far left bottom** Boating, Berlengas Archipelago

Getting to know the archipelago The Berlengas Archipelago, located 5 to 7 miles from Peniche, is made up of a group of islands and coastal reefs: Berlenga Grande, the Estelas and the Farilhões-Forcadas.

The biological richness of this place and its state of conservation earned this nature reserve the classification of World Biosphere Reserve by Unesco in 2011, including the emerged area and the marine surroundings. This unique ecosystem stands out for its endemic plants and is a protected habitat sought after by several species of seabirds for nesting.

Island's trails Berlenga Grande is the most visited island, and, in case you want to spend the night, there's a camping area (contact Posto de Turismo de Peniche to know how to reserve the tent space). Disembark at the small dock, next to the Bairro dos Pescadores 'Comandante Andrade e Silva'. It is also here that you have a stretch of sand to spread your towel and go for a dip.

Follow the walking paths around the island that lead to the **Farol do Duque de Bragança**, and the **Forte São João Baptista**, the most iconic structure on the island.

Visit the caves Book a boat and set off to discover Berlengas' geological formations. There are several caves and paths between the rocks to explore. If you are a fan of diving, be sure to do it here. The transparency of the waters and the incredible underwater life make this place unique.

🖋 Say Hello to the Common Murre!

The common murre (Uria aalge) is a seabird that spends most of the year at sea and can be seen between Iceland and Portugal. It heads for land, namely to the cliff areas, for its mating season in the wintertime.

The common murre used to breed in large numbers on Berlenga Grande and the bird is therefore the symbol of this nature reserve.

Unfortunately, since 1939, when there were an estimated 6000 pairs, there has been a decline in the presence of this species in the Berlengas, and they are now almost extinct in the archipelago.

Listings

BEST OF THE REST

👪 Family & Friends Fun

Dino Parque Lourinhã

For Jurassic fans, this park will delight the whole family. It features 180 full-scale models of dinosaur species in a theme park one hour from Lisbon.

Bacalhôa Buddha Eden

Giant Buddhas, terracotta warriors and pagodas. You will feel like you are walking through Asia in this park near Bombarral. At the end, you can also try one of the region's wines.

Óbidos Escape Tower

Walking around the walls of Óbidos Castle is a fantastic experience, but trying to escape from one of its towers is even better! This one-hour game will test your knowledge and resilience.

Parques de Sintra

Visit Sintra's historic palaces and estates, have a picnic in lush gardens or ride in a carriage paying attention to the botanical species and animals that appear along the way.

International Karting Palmela

For speed lovers, the International Karting Palmela, besides hosting international races, is perfect to try out your skills as a kart driver. You can go for a team or a speed race.

Sesimbra Safari

Wild beaches, natural pools, dinosaur footprints and socialising with locals. A complete safari-like experience to get to know the area of Sesimbra and Cabo Espichel better.

🥾 Nature Up Close

Paisagem Protegida da Serra de Montejunto

About one hour from Lisbon, this mountain range is the highest point of the West region and offers the perfect scenery for hiking and mountain biking.

Parque Natural das Serras de Aires e Candeeiros

Walk among lakes and springs, pass by old rural windmills and go underground in the Grutas de Mira de Aire. All within a little more than an hour's drive from the capital.

Mata Rainha D Leonor

The most emblematic forest of Caldas da Rainha offers 17 hectares of paths among leafy trees. Start at the Parque D Carlos I, in the city centre, and take the opportunity to visit the Bordalo Pinheiro ceramic factory.

Foz do Arelho Footbridges

An immense view over the Atlantic and the fresh sea breeze guide you on this path that stretches over the cliffs near the village of Foz do Arelho.

Bacalhôa Buddha Eden

Escarpas da Maceira

Walk along the limestone cliffs that follow the Alcabrichel river in the Vimeiro area and step on the Porto Novo beach, the same one where the British troops landed during the first Napoleonic invasion in the 19th century.

Cabo Espichel

Follow the paths that stretch along the cliffs of Cape Espichel, near Sesimbra, and take a look at the lighthouse and the Santuário de Nossa Senhora do Cabo Espichel.

Cabo Carvoeiro

At the cliffs of Cabo Carvoeiro, in Peniche, discover true geological treasures. Look for the 'cave that blows', an exit in the rock where you can feel the wind caused by the breaking waves.

Praia do Magoito

Framed by imposing cliffs, Praia do Magoito stands out for its natural beauty and strong waves breaking on a rocky bottom. Ideal for the bravest surfers.

Praias da Ursa and Adraga

Hike between Ursa and Adraga beaches for a breathtaking wild landscape. From the top, find Fojo da Adraga, a deep natural hole with a connection to the sea.

Cabo da Roca

Part of the many hiking trails you can take along the coast, Cabo da Roca is a must-see. In what is the westernmost point of Europe; see the 1772 lighthouse and look for the cross with Camões' words.

Lagoa Azul

This beautiful lagoon, a 20-minute drive from Cabo da Roca in Sintra, is the perfect place for a romantic picnic or nature hike.

Praia do Magoito

🍷 Sweets & Wine

Capinha d'Óbidos €€

Delicious squeezed juices, freshly baked bread with regional chorizo, and Ferraduras, the typical cakes of the house. Everything goes into the picnic basket prepared by Capinha d'Óbidos, next to Praça de Santa Maria.

Oppidum €

Learn the secrets of the most famous Ginginha de Óbidos with a visit to the Oppidum factory, one of the oldest producers of this liquor. In Sobral da Lagoa, 10 minutes from the town of Óbidos.

Adega Cooperativa da Lourinhã €€

From these cellars comes the Aguardente DOC 'Lourinhã', which is one of the only three demarcated wine brandy regions in Europe. Discover, taste and take back home.

Pastelaria Regional do Cego €

Established in 1901, this pastry shop has been passed down from generation to generation. The famous Tortas de Azeitão are the flagship of this house in Vila Nogueira de Azeitão, 20 minutes from Setúbal.

Casa Piriquita €

Almost as famous as the Palácio da Pena. Since 1862 Casa Piriquita has been serving the famous Travesseiros de Sintra, a cake made of a light puff pastry and an egg and almond cream filling.

Adega Regional de Colares €€

Take a guided tour with a winemaker to get to know one of the oldest cooperative wineries in Portugal. In Colares, 40 minutes from Lisbon.

Adega Viúva Gomes €€

Influenced by the sea and the Serra de Sintra, this winery in Colares invites you to taste its wines' fresh and saline flavours.

Casa Ermelinda Freitas €€

Learn about the production process of one of the best-known wines of the Setúbal Peninsula with a visit to Casa Ermelinda Freitas, near Palmela.

⚓ Water Exploration

Feeling Berlenga

From visits to the Berlenga caves to dolphin watching or a diving baptism. The Feeling Berlenga boat departs from the Peniche Fishing Port.

Lagoa de Albufeira

Get in the water of this National Ecological Reserve for a session of stand-up paddle boarding, kite surfing or windsurfing. Right next to it, take a dip in the sea.

Intertidal

Explore Lagoa de Óbidos by kayak on a scientific tour, accompanied by a marine specialist who helps you identify marine organisms, algae, and even edible plants.

Dolphin Bay

Setúbal's bay explored in detail. Choose the one-day program that includes dolphin-watching, accompanied by marine biologists, touring the main points of interest in Arrábida, and a stop for a meal and snorkelling.

🐟 Fish & Seafood Lovers

Casa Santiago €

Known as 'the king of fried cuttlefish', this is the perfect place to try Setúbal's traditional dish. It is usually very crowded, so go early.

Cais da Praia €€

The fresh seafood that comes out of the Lagoa de Óbidos makes its way directly to the tables here; it also stands out for its cocktail menu.

Tibino €€

With decor based on details and artworks by local artists, try the clams cooked *à bulhão pato* or the fried eels, among other delicacies to die for, in this Foz do Arelho 'snack house'.

Solar dos Amigos €€€

In a small town called Guisado, in the Caldas da Rainha area, this traditional restaurant is known for its generous portions and an enviable showcase of desserts at the end. Try the codfish *tiborna*.

Casa Piriquita

Tasca do Joel €€

A Peniche classic and, for many, the best restaurant in town. The fish and seafood options are abundant here, as are the suggestions on the wine list.

A Sardinha €€

For fresh fish caught off the coast of Peniche or more traditional dishes such as *caldeirada*, seafood *cataplana* or monkfish rice. Five minutes from Forte de Peniche.

Azenhas do Mar €€€

Lobster, scallops, scarlet shrimps, oysters or a variety of fresh fish. All with one of the best views of the Sintra coast. Enjoy a swim in the natural pool and stay for the sunset.

A Tasquinha €€

In the coastal resort of Nazaré, this friendly family affair has been running for 50-plus years, serving high-quality seafood in a pair of snug but prettily tiled dining rooms.

Scenic Routes

Sintra-Praia das Maçãs Tram

Take the historic tram that connects Sintra to Praia das Maçãs. The 10km route is divided between Sintra's lush landscape and the proximity to the sea.

Cabo da Roca Road

Between Praia do Guincho and Cabo da Roca, the westernmost point of mainland Portugal, stretches a road of twists and turns filled with the beauty of the Parque Natural de Sintra.

ALLARD ONE/SHUTTERSTOCK ©

Historic tram, Sintra

 **History Tracker**

Roman Ruins of Tróia

It was one of the largest fish salting sites in the Roman Empire and the Western Mediterranean, and its ruins can be visited in Tróia, a boat ride away from Setúbal.

Fortaleza de Peniche

This fort gained a reputation in Portugal's democratic history by being turned into a political prison during the fascist regime. Visit the exhibits inside and be impressed by the view from the bastion.

Castelo de Palmela

Climb up to Castelo de Palmela for an incredible view of the vineyards that produce some of Portugal's best wines, the Serra da Arrábida, and the bay of Setúbal.

11
Seeking Spirituality in
THE CENTRO

HISTORY | RELIGION | PILGRIMAGE

███████ Myths, mystery and spirituality define this two-day route through the captivating Centro region. Discover the history of the Knights Templar and Reconquista period in Portugal, marvel at magnificent monasteries, and pray at, or respect, the nation's leading pilgrimage site of Fátima.

NAUGHTYNUT/SHUTTERSTOCK ©

🗺 Trip Notes

Getting here Driving will mean a quicker journey. Local buses (rodotejo.pt) and CP trains provide access to most stops.

When to go Major mass celebrations occur in Fátima on 13 May and 13 October. Time travel in Tomar on select dates in July for the Templar Festival.

Extend your trip Visit Unesco-listed Alcobaça Monastery, or Castelo Branco, where the remains of a Templar castle rise above the city.

🏰 The Knights Templar

Headquartered in Tomar, the Knights Templar settled in Portugal during the 12th-century, playing a crucial role in the Christian Reconquest of the nation. Gualdim Pais, the founder of Tomar, oversaw the construction of other castle strongholds, such as Almourol, Monsanto and Pombal.

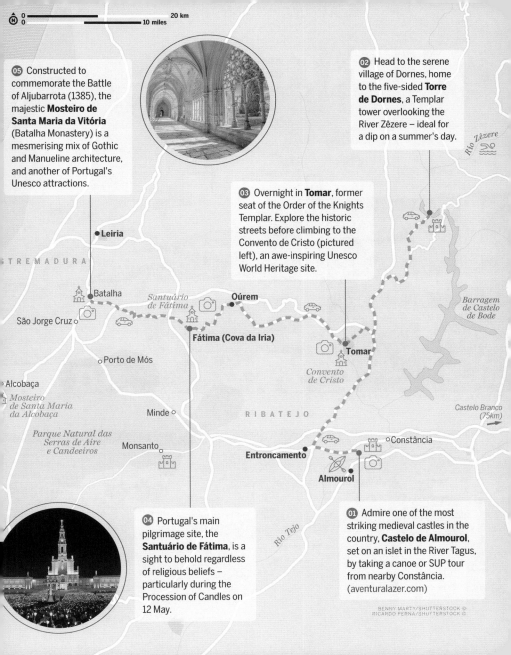

05 Constructed to commemorate the Battle of Aljubarrota (1385), the majestic **Mosteiro de Santa Maria da Vitória** (Batalha Monastery) is a mesmerising mix of Gothic and Manueline architecture, and another of Portugal's Unesco attractions.

02 Head to the serene village of Dornes, home to the five-sided **Torre de Dornes**, a Templar tower overlooking the River Zêzere – ideal for a dip on a summer's day.

03 Overnight in **Tomar**, former seat of the Order of the Knights Templar. Explore the historic streets before climbing to the Convento de Cristo (pictured left), an awe-inspiring Unesco World Heritage site.

04 Portugal's main pilgrimage site, the **Santuário de Fátima**, is a sight to behold regardless of religious beliefs – particularly during the Procession of Candles on 12 May.

01 Admire one of the most striking medieval castles in the country, **Castelo de Almourol**, set on an islet in the River Tagus, by taking a canoe or SUP tour from nearby Constância. (aventuralazer.com)

20 km
10 miles

Río Zêzere

Leiria

ESTREMADURA

Batalha

São Jorge Cruz

Santuário de Fátima

Oúrem

Fátima (Cova da Iria)

Porto de Mós

Alcobaça

Mosteiro de Santa Maria da Alcobaça

Minde

Parque Natural das Serras de Aire e Candeeiros

Monsanto

Barragem de Castelo de Bode

Tomar

Convento de Cristo

RIBATEJO

Castelo Branco (75km)

Entroncamento

Almourol

Constância

Río Tejo

ALENTEJO

HISTORY | VILLAGES | WINE

Experience
Alentejo
online

ALENTEJO
Trip Builder

Wherever you are – by the seaside, sitting under a tree or standing atop a castle overlooking the mountains with a wine or gin to hand – the Alentejo invites you to slow down and enjoy its diverse scenery.

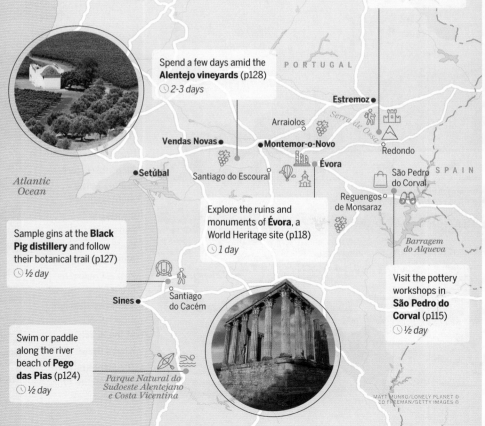

0 — 40 km
0 — 20 miles

Climb up castles and hike along the valleys of **Serra de Ossa** (p111)
⏱ *1-2 days*

Spend a few days amid the **Alentejo vineyards** (p128)
⏱ *2-3 days*

PORTUGAL

Estremoz ●

Arraiolos ○

Serra de Ossa

Vendas Novas ●

● **Montemor-o-Novo**

● Setúbal

Santiago do Escoural

● **Évora**

Redondo

São Pedro do Corval

S P A I N

Reguengos de Monsaraz ○

Atlantic Ocean

Sample gins at the **Black Pig distillery** and follow their botanical trail (p127)
⏱ *½ day*

Explore the ruins and monuments of **Évora**, a World Heritage site (p118)
⏱ *1 day*

Barragem do Alqueva

Sines ●

Santiago do Cacém

Visit the pottery workshops in **São Pedro do Corval** (p115)
⏱ *½ day*

Swim or paddle along the river beach of **Pego das Pias** (p124)
⏱ *½ day*

Parque Natural do Sudoeste Alentejano e Costa Vicentina

Practicalities

TOP: A5 FOOD STUDIO/SHUTTERSTOCK ®
BOTTOM: NATALIASPB/GETTY IMAGES ©

ALENTEJO FIND YOUR FEET

ARRIVING

Lisbon & Faro Airports Lisbon to reach the coast and Évora; Faro for villages further south.

Évora is home to Alentejo's main train station and bus terminal, offering connections to smaller towns.

FIND YOUR WAY

Local tourist offices provide guides and maps. See rotavicentina.com for details about the coastal trails.

MONEY

Many restaurants offer lunch deals; some only accept cash. Note: entrées aren't usually free (and it's fine to turn them down).

WHERE TO STAY

Location	Atmosphere
Évora	Alentejo's capital city; guesthouses and hotels housed in former convents
Vila Nova de Milfontes	Country houses, beachside hotels; best for hiking the Rota Vicentina and surfing
Comporta	Luxurious ecoresorts amid the dunes; spas, horse riding and dolphin-watching
Monsaraz	Rural estates and stylish guesthouses overlooking vineyards; ideal for stargazing

EATING & DRINKING

Açorda Bread soup topped with poached eggs, garlic, olive oil and coriander or pennyroyal.

Porco Preto The Iberian black pig is a quintessential Alentejo ingredient served in a variety of cuts.

Migas Breadcrumbs are mixed with vegetables and/or pork fat to create this filling side dish.

Must-try dessert
Taberna do Adro's *sericaia* (p131)

Best wine experience
Herdade da Malhadinha Nova (p129)

GETTING AROUND

Driving is the best way to reach the vineyards and the smallest villages.

Trains connect the Sete Rios station in Lisbon with Alentejo's capital, Évora.

Buses are ideal to reach small cities and towns where the train does not go.

JAN–MAR	APR–JUN	JUL–SEP	OCT–DEC
Moderate temperatures, perfect for trying hearty Alentejo dishes	Fine weather and blooming flowers, ideal for hiking	Long hot days for swimming and to join the wine harvest	Cooler weather and some rainy days, good for visiting museums

12 Step into
HISTORY

CASTLES | NATURE | VILLAGES

Whitewashed houses nestled amid the countryside, castles overlooking mountains or river valleys and endless nature trails: Alentejo's byways are worth every detour. Seemingly quiet on the surface, the region's ancient towns have been reinvigorated by a slew of new attractions and diversions, from sailing in Europe's largest artificial lake to cycling along disused train tracks.

IAKOV FILIMONOV/SHUTTERSTOCK ©

🗺 How to

Getting around Some villages are accessible by bus from Évora or Beja, others are best reached by car. Rede Expressos serves the big cities, while Rodoviária do Alentejo covers smaller areas.

When to go Avoid the scorching sun but still make the most of the activities in spring or early autumn.

Follow the train tracks Pedal along old railway tracks connecting the villages of Marvão and Castelo de Vide with Rail Bike Marvão (railbike marvao.com).

RJC9666/SHUTTERSTOCK ©

Castles, villages & ruins The battle days are long gone, but the castles and forts built against invaders remain, from the circular battlements of **Arraiolos** and **Évoramonte** to the fully walled towns of **Marvão** and **Monsaraz**. Close to the Spanish border, Marvão stands out with its majestic castle hovering above the São Mamede Natural Park. Visit in the summer for a swim on the nearby beach of Portagem or catch the classical-music festival held inside the castle. In Monsaraz, you'll find most of the region's wineries, making it the perfect base for wine tastings. The Unesco city of **Elvas** also makes the list with its star-shaped bulwarks. While in **Alcácer do Sal** and **Estremoz**, castles have been turned into luxury hotels. Down south, you can explore the whitewashed streets of **Serpa**, stopping for a tasting at one of the local cheesemongers, the perfect fuel for your climb up to the castle, or head to **Mértola** to visit Islamic ruins and sail along the Guadiana river. On your way there, visit the waterfall of **Pulo do Lobo**. Roman ruins are also a common sight in the Alentejo, including the **Ruínas de São Cucufate** and the **Villa Romana de Pisões**.

Nature trails The 3.6km **Barca d'Amieira trail** near Nisa offers views across the Tejo river, a suspended footbridge and swings, while in Redondo, wooden walkways take you across the valleys of **Serra de Ossa**.

Far left top Forte da Graça, Elvas
Far left bottom Castelo de Arraiolos

☆ Sailing under the Stars

Close to Monsaraz is the Alqueva Dam, the largest artificial lake in Europe, where you can spend days on end swimming or sailing. This is also the first region in the world to become a Starlight Tourism Destination. The lack of light noise offers the perfect conditions for stargazing. Take in the night sky with your own eyes or visit the **Observatório Lago Alqueva** (olagoalqueva. pt) for guided sightings.

Culture of the Alentejo

EMBRACE THE FLOW IN PORTUGAL'S LARGEST REGION

Time seems to pause as you set foot in the Alentejo. The vast golden meadows with their lonesome cork and olive trees and the slow-paced lifestyle mastered by the *alentejanos* feels miles away from the modern world. There's an art to living this way and people are taking notice.

There's an invitation to slow down in the Alentejo. Even the word *'devagar'*, the Portuguese term for slow, feels longer than most, especially when pronounced with the Alentejo accent. Unlike the speedy speaking pace of the big cities, the *alentejanos* take time prolonging their vowels.

What used to be a running joke among the urban dwellers is now a cherished character for those contemplating a slower lifestyle. Through the centuries, the Alentejo has managed to keep most of its traditions alive, with its rustic cuisine, handmade crafts and winemaking techniques. Just like baking the Alentejo bread, every art here takes time, from the embedded stone drawings of Nisa's ceramics to the thread weaving of the Arraiolos tapestries.

A recent campaign by the local winery Herdade do Esporão embraces this unhurried approach. *'Feito devagar no* Alentejo' (Made slowly in the Alentejo) was launched in early 2021 and provides a parallel between their winemaking process and the time-honoured practices of local artisans.

Even those oak trees that are quintessential of the Alentejo take 25 years to produce cork. The numbers you'll see engraved on each tree recall the date of harvest, which only happens every eight to nine years. Around June, local men strip off the trees with their delicate axe skills, a work of mastery since a bad cut can result in killing the tree. Outsiders are invited to explore these fields – on foot or in a bumpy all-terrain vehicle – through an experience known as Corktrekking.

Left Alentejo vineyard workers
Middle Praia do Comporta **Right** Cork oak and bark

ANJO KAN/SHUTTERSTOCK ©

Portugal is one of the world's biggest cork producers, and while most of it ends up sealing your bottle of wine, locals have found other creative purposes for this sustainable material, using it to make anything from coasters to shoes and umbrellas. There are even hotels using cork for their walls.

For a few days or weeks, you can experience a slice of countryside life with activities such as olive harvesting, fishing or horse riding, and some swimming breaks in between. You can linger on the beach close to Comporta or venture deep into the countryside to places such as Albernoa or Redondo.

> Through the centuries, the Alentejo has managed to keep most of its traditions alive, with its rustic cuisine, handmade crafts and winemaking techniques.

A global trend towards slow-living and remote life has drawn many visitors to this region, a place that has always been renowned for its rural estates known as *montes* or *herdades*, some of which have now been revamped by award-winning local architects such as Álvaro Siza Vieira or Eduardo Souto de Moura.

Some have been so taken by Alentejo's laid-back lifestyle that they've bought a second home here, such as fashion designer Christian Louboutin, and for many Portuguese, there's a lingering dream of retiring here.

♘ Horseback Pilgrimage

Mounted on horses, hundreds ride from Moita to Viana do Alentejo on this large equestrian pilgrimage held in late April. The Romaria a Cavalo started in the 19th century when Moita's farmers rode to the Nossa Senhora d'Aires Sanctuary in Viana praying for good crops. After a nearly 70-year break, the pilgrimage returned in 2001, attracting visitors from all over the country. It takes four days to cover the 150km trail across the rural fields, and on arrival participants are welcomed with live music and dance performances.

13 Crafting a
MOVEMENT

ART | CULTURE | TRADITION

Folk-style furniture, hand-woven tapestries and painted ceramics: Alentejo's tradtional craftwork trades are kept alive through a circle of artisans who have turned their towns into colourful art hubs. Even the labourers' anthem that once echoed through the fields is now part of this cultural movement. Museums, crafty villages and workshops: here are Alentejo's creative nooks.

CHRISTIAN GOUPI/ALAMY STOCK PHOTO ©

🗺 How to

Getting around It's possible to visit some of the art towns, such as Portalegre and Estremoz, by bus; others are best reached by car or with a guided tour.

When to go Summer is a good time to catch craft fairs and festivals.

Getting crafty Meet local artisans and join traditional craft workshops with the guides of the Portugal Heritage Tours.

JOSERPIZARRO/SHUTTERSTOCK ©

Left Ceramic production, São Pedro do Corval **Far left top** Fábrica Alentejana de Lanifícios **Far left bottom** Craft store, Estremoz

ALENTEJO EXPERIENCES

Art towns & fading crafts The Alentejo is home to the country's largest pottery centre, **São Pedro do Corval**, but other towns like **Viana do Alentejo** and **Nisa** are also ceramic hubs. Nisa is especially famous for its embroidery-like motifs made with quartz, which have inspired the redesign of one of its streets in 2021 with red and white cobblestones. In **Estremoz**, the jazzy Bonecos de Estremoz are the first figurines to be recognised as Cultural Heritage. Nearby, **Arraiolos** produces intricate rugs with Moorish influences, while in **Portalegre**, tapestries reproduce paintings. Further south, in **Monsaraz** and **Mértola** you'll find hand-woven blankets once used to warm local herders. Other crafts are slowly fading, such as the Pintura Alentejana, a furniture-painting style with floral motifs, and the Chocalhos, metal bells hand-crafted in **Alcáçovas** and used by farmers to distinguish their herds. The lack of artisans in this field has made it an endangered craft.

The music of a revolution When 'Grândola, Vila Morena' was broadcast on Portuguese radio in 1974, it signalled a revolution that ended a dictatorship era lasting nearly 50 years. This song is an ode to the Cante Alentejano, a music genre that has its roots in the Alentejo fields. Once sung by local farmers, this slow-paced a cappella tune can still be heard in small taverns and local associations. It's been a Unesco patrimony since 2014.

🏺 Workshops & Museums

Olaria Bulhão Purchase hand-painted ceramics or join a workshop at this small atelier in Corval.

Artesanato Zézinha One of the few places still producing the Alentejo-style furniture.

Museu das Tapeçarias de Portalegre Giant tapestries decorate the walls of this fabulous Portalegre museum.

Centro Interpretativo do Tapete de Arraiolos Learn the history of the Arraiolos tapestries and take home a mini rug kit.

Fábrica Alentejana de Lanifícios Colourful hand-loomed woollen blankets hang within this Monsaraz factory.

Oficina de Tecelagem de Mértola Peek inside this weaving workshop near the church of Mértola.

Irmãs Flores An atelier dedicated to the Bonecos de Estremoz run by a sister-duo.

CRAFTS
of the Alentejo

01 Tapetes de Arraiolos

Embroidery wool rugs produced in Arraiolos, a tradition inherited by the Moors who settled here around the 16th century.

02 Mantas Alentejanas

Multicoloured woollen blankets made around Mértola or Monsaraz, currently used in Portuguese homes as bed throws or rugs.

03 Pintura Alentejana

Red, blue and green are the traditional colours used in this painted furniture style famous for its floral motifs.

04 Cante Alentejano

For special performances of Cante Alentejano, singers put on a traditional attire that includes a hat, vest and scarf.

05 Capote Alentejano

Wool cloak with a fur collar, usually made of fox or sheepskin, once used to warm the local shepherds.

06 Cork Products

The Alentejo is renowned for its cork and some is used to produce fashion

items such as bags, hats,
shoes and wallets.

07 Chocalhos

Dating back 2000 years,
these metal rattles
used to be a common
sound in the Alentejo,
but they're slowly
disappearing.

08 Bonecos
de Estremoz

Colourful handcrafted
bonecas (clay figures)
produced in Estremoz.
Saints are common
motifs, as well as the
'primaveras', women
with flowers around
their heads.

09 Tapeçarias
de Portalegre

Paintings can be
replicated into
stunning hand-woven
pieces thanks to the
intricate stitch used
in the Portalegre-style
tapestries.

10 Olaria Pedrada
de Nisa

In Nisa, ceramicists
are known as the
'bordadeiras de pedra'
(stone embroiderers) as
they use bits of quartz
to adorn the clay.

Past & Present in
ÉVORA

DAY TRIP | HISTORY | RUINS

A time capsule of Portugal's past, the city of Évora has earned its World Heritage status. Here, Neolithic monuments stand alongside Roman ruins and Gothic churches embellished with blue-and-white tiles. As the capital of the Alentejo, Évora is the perfect starting point for a tour of the region.

ANDRES NAGA/SHUTTERSTOCK ©

🗺 How to

Getting here & around A train from Lisbon to Évora takes about 1½ hours. You can cover most of the attractions on foot, except the megalithic sites, which are best reached on a tour.

When to go Spring and early autumn are the best times to avoid the heat but still enjoy sunny days.

Pastry stop Try traditional conventual sweets at Pastelaria Conventual Pão de Rala, such as *queijadas* or *pão de rala*.

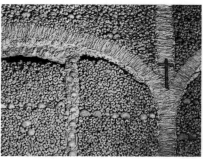

SAIKO3P/SHUTTERSTOCK ©

Left Display of pre-historic objects, Ebora Megalithica **Far left top** Templo Romano, Évora **Far left bottom** Igreja de São Francisco, Évora

Find your Route

Prehistory Évora's early origins can be traced to **Alto de São Bento**, once one of the largest prehistoric villages in the region, and now a favourite spot for sunsets. The **Centro Interpretativo dos Almendres** is the meeting point for tours of the surrounding menhirs, far older than Stonehenge, and hosts prehistoric-themed workshops. Think firing arrows, ceramics, and hand-carving stone plaques.

Roman gems Traces of the Romans' presence are still visible in the **Templo Romano** and the thermal baths uncovered beneath the city council. The **Museu de Évora** holds many of the relics discovered in the region.

Bones, frescoes & tiles The **Igreja de São Francisco** intrigues visitors with its eerie bone chapel, while the **Igreja dos Lóios** stands out with its tile-covered interior. For panoramic views of the city, make sure to climb up to the cathedral's terrace. Since you're nearby, don't miss the animal frescoes hidden within the **Centro de Arte e Cultura**.

Fly, hike or cycle Jump out of a plane and glide above the Alentejo clouds with a skydiving experience offered at the **Aeródromo de Évora** or ride a hot-air balloon and enjoy incredible views over the meadows and church spires. Rather keep your feet on the ground? You can follow a section of the **Santiago pilgrimage route** (caminhosdesantiagoalentejo ribatejo.pt) or cycle along the **Ecopista de Évora**, stopping for a glass of wine at the **Fitapreta vineyard**.

Megalithic Évora

The confluence of the rivers Tejo, Sado and Guadiana and the abundance of granite outcrops made Évora an ideal settlement for the Neolithic people. These farmer communities were the first *alentejanos*, the ones that cultivated the land and domesticated the animals, a tradition that is still alive today through the region's shepherds. Of the remaining Neolithic sites, the Cromeleque dos Almendres stands out as one of the largest megalithic settlements in Europe, but the Anta Grande do Zambujeiro and the Gruta do Escoural are also worth visiting.

Mário Carvalho,
archaeologist at
Ebora Megalithica
@ebora_megalithica

A Journey through Time

**LAYERS OF
PORTUGAL'S PAST
UNFOLD IN ÉVORA**

Since becoming a Unesco Heritage site, Alentejo's sleepy capital has gained global recognition. But Roman emperors and Portuguese kings saw Évora's appeal centuries ago when they settled here. From royal getaway to the rise of the inquisition, here's how Évora has switched roles through the years.

Left Praça do Giraldo **Middle**
Suovetaurilia illustration **Right**
Palácio de Dom Manuel

SAIKO3P/SHUTTERSTOCK ©

Every city has a meeting point. In Évora, all streets lead to Praça do Giraldo. Under the square's arcades, shops and cafes draw locals, while travellers take turns capturing the surrounding neoclassical buildings. Many forget that this was also the birthplace of the Portuguese Inquisition, a dark chapter recalled only by a victim's memorial, placed here in 2016. Following the pope's approval, in the 16th century, crowds gathered in Praça do Giraldo for the so-called *autos-da-fé*, a public penance ritual that started in Évora and soon took the country by storm.

Long before the royal family and the Inquisition landed in Évora, the city was occupied by the Romans, who nicknamed it *Ebora Liberalitas Julia*. While many buildings were destroyed after the country's conversion to Christianity, one managed to survive thanks to its medieval role as the city's butchers. That monument is the infamous Roman temple, Évora's most iconic site and one of the reasons why the city secured its Unesco Heritage title. The temple was part of a larger forum and was used as a place for animal sacrifices known as the *suovetaurilia*. This wasn't far off from its future position as a butcher's shop, where meat was cut and distributed to the people. The exposed stone columns that you see today were hidden under plaster and it was only in the 19th century that locals realised the value of this building and took the walls down. Traces of the Romans are also visible in the city's ancient arches and in the latest discovery of the thermal baths underneath the town hall in 1987.

By the 15th century, Évora had become a favourite getaway for the Portuguese royal family. Kings and queens built their palaces here and other noble families followed

suit. In Palácio de Dom Manuel, royal babies were born, while theatrical performances took over the stage. Among the last performances enacted here was a piece by the Portuguese poet Gil Vicente. *Villancicos* were also common, and a compilation of these polyphonic tunes was launched in 2014 by the musical group A Corte Musical. As for the palace, like many others in Évora, it's being converted into an exhibition space.

> Long before the royal family and the Inquisition landed in Évora, the city was occupied by the Romans, who nicknamed it *Ebora Liberalitas Julia*.

Not long after the royal family's arrival, Évora established its university in 1559, the second oldest in Portugal, followed by Coimbra. Originally run by the Jesuits, it was sadly targeted by Marquês de Pombal (1699–1782), who ordered the school's closing in 1779 following a period of Jesuit oppression, which swept across Europe in the Age of Enlightenment. Teachers were sent into exile or incarcerated, and the doors were closed for nearly two centuries. It was only in 1973 that it reopened, giving the young population of the Alentejo a chance to sign up to university without moving too far from home. Today, these students are the living soul of Évora.

♨ A Roman Bath

If you've ever wanted to experience a Roman thermal bath, head to the **In Acqua Veritas Spa** (inacquaveritas. com) just a few steps off Praça do Giraldo. This spa tries to recreate the Roman baths' setting and is the only one of its kind in Portugal. Like the ancient baths, this one consists of three pools at different temperatures: the *tepidarium* (warm water at around 32°C), the *caldarium* (very hot water around 40°C) and the *frigidarium* (cold water around 16°C). It's also possible to book massages or enjoy tea and wine in their winter garden.

15 At the
BEACH

BEACHES | HIKING | SURFING

Horse riding along the sand, surfing at a secluded beach or hiking one of Portugal's best coastal trails: visitors can find it all amid the sea and the river dams scattered across the Alentejo.

ALEXANDER SPATARI/GETTY IMAGES ©

ALENTEJO EXPERIENCES

How to

Getting here Coastal towns like Vila Nova de Milfontes and Sines are accessible by bus from Lisbon or the Algarve; other areas are best reached by car.

When to go Weather is best in late spring and summer, but visiting off-season means you'll often have the beach to yourself.

Island trip Hop on a boat and go snorkelling off Ilha do Pessegueiro, a small island off the coast of Porto Covo. Trips only available in the summer.

OLGA KOBERIDZE/SHUTTERSTOCK ©

Beaches

By the sea A string of wild and secluded beaches surround the coast of the Alentejo. Here, it's still possible to find an empty patch of sand even in the height of summer. Get on a horse and ride along the dunes at **Praia da Comporta**, a beach that has attracted the likes of Madonna and Christian Louboutin. Dolphins can often be spotted around here and along the Troia peninsula. Don't miss a visit to the nearby **Cais Palafítico da Carrasqueira**, a fishermen's port carefully balanced on stilts.

Head to **Porto Covo** or **Sines** for the best wave action or paddle your way to the beaches of **Vila Nova de Milfontes**. SURFaddict Association (surfadaptado.pt) can help people with disabilities to experience the waves.

JULIAN GAZZARD/SHUTTERSTOCK ©

꧁ Midsummer Party

Music festivals liven up the Alentejo coast around July and August. Dance to world music at the **Festival Músicas do Mundo** in Sines or head to Zambujeira do Mar for **MEO Sudoeste** and enjoy a swim in the canal between sets.

Left Cais Palafítico da Carrasqueira **Above left** Praia do Malhão, Vila Nova de Milfontes **Above right** Ilha do Pessegueiro

At **Praia da Samoqueira**, picturesque natural pools emerge at low tide, and further south the **Praia do Cavaleiro** is one of the region's smallest coves, near Cape Sardão, the perfect sunset spot.

Rivers & dams The region's rivers and dams have created many inland beaches. There's **Praia Fluvial do Gameiro** with its riverside walkway and the idyllic waters of **Pego das Pias** near Odemira. It's around here that you'll find the **Santa Clara Dam**, a great fishing site.

Near the Spanish border, you can join a boat trip across the **Alqueva Dam** or relax at the **Praia Fluvial de Monsaraz**, which features both sand and grassy areas, as well as wheelchair access. In Mértola, within the Guadiana Natural Park is the **Albufeira da Tapada Grande**, close to the now-abandoned mining site of São Domingos.

Alentejo's Best Surfing Spots

L-Point, Porto Covo
Portugal's most fun wave, ideal for goofy foots. Three sections with room for creativity, where it's still possible to surf alone sometimes.

Lagoa de Santo André
A concealed wave, which is either epic or so bad you can't surf. You need to combine the winds and swell with the perfect opening of the lagoon to the sea, and then the tubes will come.

Pico Louco, São Torpes
One of Alentejo's most popular waves. Versatile peak, with easy but powerful rights and lefts, rolling over a partially sand-covered rock shelf.

Recommended by
João Kopke,
professional surfer
@joaokopke

Santiago do Cacém

Sines

Atlantic Ocean

BAIXO ALENTEJO

Rio Sado

Cercal

Vila Nova de Milfontes

Parque Natural do Sudoeste Alentejano e Costa Vicentina

Pego das Pias

Cavaleiro
Praia do Cavaleiro

Odemira

Santa Clara

Zambujeira do Mar

Santa-Clara-a-Velha

Santa Clara Dam

São Teotónio

20 km
10 miles

Left Lagoa de Santo André
Below Parque Natural do Sudoeste Alentejano e Costa Vicentina

Coastal Trails & Villages

Nature lovers will enjoy hiking or cycling across the region's natural reserves. The **Sado Estuary** is the ideal place to spot dolphins and flamingos, but the area's biggest draw is the **Costa Vicentina**, a coastal park that stretches all the way to the Algarve. The 230km **Historical Way** is the longest route and passes through small towns like Porto Covo. The **Fishermen's Trail**, although shorter at around 125km, is more demanding as it takes you along the windswept cliffs. Circular routes allow for shorter walks of half a day or less, so don't let the numbers scare you off. Spring and autumn are the best times to follow these trails to avoid the heat. See rotavicentina.com for more info.

Along the way, it's worth stopping at some of the region's charming villages such as **Zambujeira do Mar**. Arrive early in the morning and head to **Entrada da Barca** to see the fishermen returning from their catch on colourful wooden boats. A bit further inland, the **Aldeia de Santa Susana** and **Santa-Clara-a-Velha** stand out with their iconic houses framed in white and blue.

16

What's
BREWING

DAY TRIP | GIN | LIQUORS

Sweet fruit liquors, gins and rum: this land yields much more than wine. In between vineyards, there is an abundant flora that has captivated a new generation of distillers. Many have opened their doors allowing you to sample some of the region's top tipples straight from the source.

SILVAPINTO1985/GETTY IMAGES ©

🗺 **How to**

Getting around Most of the distilleries are located in small towns on the outskirts, so the best way to reach them is to drive.

When to go Distilleries are open year-round, but spring and early autumn are the ideal seasons to observe the botanicals in full bloom.

Nature hike Follow the Charneca de São Teotónio trail, an 8.5km circular route that passes through fields of *medronheiros* (strawberry trees).

STEPHEN BARNES/PORTUGAL/ALAMY STOCK PHOTO ©

SERGIO SERGIO/SHUTTERSTOCK ©

Left Medronho berries **Far left top** Gin cocktail **Far left bottom** Medronho distillation pot

Liquor & medronho At 42%, a glass of *medronho* isn't for the faint-hearted, but this regional firewater is a staple in many Portuguese bars. Learn how to make it at the **Museu do Medronho** or in the small town of Almodôvar, where a football field is being converted into a mini *medronho* hub. New distilleries like **Junior Jacques** are also reimagining this fiery drink, which is the base for many fruit liqueurs. Acorn liquor is quite popular, as well as cherry and *poejo* (pennyroyal).

Gin Gin is taking over the Alentejo. There's the **Destilaria Monte da Bica**, a winery-turned-distillery near Montemor-o-Novo. In Monsaraz, the **Sharish Gin** stands out with its colour-changing gin, Blue Magic: a blue drink that turns pink when mixed with tonic water. By the coast is **Black Pig**, with its award-winning gin. Beyond a distillery, this is a thematic park offering safari trips on giant gin bottles, a cocktail bar, and a 3km trail, which takes visitors on a walk through the botanicals used in their gin.

Rum The small Alentejo island of Ilha do Pessegueiro and its pirate tales inspired the creation of a local rum. Most Portuguese rum comes from Madeira, but in 2019 the Black Pig distillery launched the first rum of mainland Portugal. The molasses still comes from Madeira but it's infused with coffee grains, peaches, tobacco leaves and vanilla, all grown on-site.

The Art of Gin-Making

Unlike wine with its distinct grapes and terroir, making gin is like music, with every producer adding their own spin to it. Sourcing local ingredients is our top priority, but others are happy mixing and matching botanicals, which is what makes Alentejo's gin so diverse. More than a producer, I feel like an alchemist of fragrances, capturing the essence of the Alentejo coast and my grandparent's land. From the dunes, we collect the juniper berries, the base of every gin, and from there we add an infusion of endemic botanicals and fruits grown on our property. They said gin was a passing trend, but we're still here.

Miguel Nunes,
alchemist at Black Pig Gin
@blackpig_gin

17

The Alentejo
UNCORKED

WINE | HISTORY | DAY TRIP

▬▬▬ While it's hard to pinpoint who brought wine to the party, records show that Phoenicians, Greeks and Romans all drank their share when they landed in the Alentejo. With plenty of sun, light winds and flatlands, this has proven to be the ideal spot for vine-growing. So grab a glass and get ready to experience one of Portugal's best wine regions.

PER KARLSSON, BKWINE 2/ALAMY STOCK PHOTO ©

🗺 **How to**

Getting around There are some vineyards near Évora and Beja, but most are located in rural lands on the outskirts. It's best to drive there or arrange a guided tour.

When to go Visit in early summer for a tour in milder temperatures or come around early autumn to catch the *vindimas* (grape harvest). September is the ideal time to join the barefoot stomping.

Stay among the vines Spend the night at the **L'and Vineyards** and enjoy spa treatments using regional grapes and wines.

HORACIO VILLALOBOS/GETTY IMAGES ©

FRANCISCO NOGUEIRA ©

Left Fitapreta vineyard **Far left top**
Herdade da Malhadinha Nova **Far left
bottom** Adega Mayor

A bittersweet tale Wine production was already here when
the Romans settled, but they turned it up a notch. With the
arrival of the Moors it was cut short, a dry spell that lasted
for centuries. The vineyards flourished again in the 1500s,
only to be left behind once more with Marquês de Pombal's
leaning towards the Douro region. Doubly so after Salazar's
(1889–1970) campaign to turn the Alentejo into the country's
breadbasket, uprooting vineyards in favour of grain and wheat.
Even with fewer plots, the Alentejo vineyards continued thanks
to those small producers who stuck to it, and today almost
half of the country's production comes from here.

Know your wine Alentejo's balmy climate is ideal for grape
ripening, but the coolness of the mountains brings diversity
to its wines. Alentejo is renowned for its reds, full-bodied with
black fruit aromas, but there's been a recent move towards
whites with smooth tropical hints. The *castas* (grape varieties)
are often mixed to create a well-balanced blend. Head towards
Campo Maior for a yoga class with wine at the **Adega Mayor** or
join a wine course at **Herdade da Malhadinha Nova** near Beja.
In Vidigueira, **Honrado Vineyards** produces *Vinho de Talha*, a
wine aged in a ceramic amphora, as the Romans did over 2000
years ago. **Fitapreta**, in Évora, is among the few producing a
white version of this wine. It's also around here that you'll find
the **Alentejo Wine Route** headquarters (vinhosdoalentejo.pt).

Classic & Up-&-Coming Wineries

Herdade do Mouchão
A classic for red wines,
pairs well with *secretos de
porco*, a traditional grilled
pork dish.

Quinta do Mouro Another
high-rated red, produced
in mostly unirrigated
schist soils around
Estremoz.

Dona Maria Júlio Bastos
Traditional foot treading
in marble mills and old
castas result in potent red
wines.

Fitapreta Long-lost
grapes such as Tamarez
and Alicante-Branco
bloom once more at this
Évora winery.

Adega do Monte Branco
Deep red wines by a fairly
recent winery created by
Luís Louro.

Susana Esteban Up-and-
coming white wines hail-
ing from the mountains of
Portalegre.

Recommended by
António Maçanita,
winemaker at Fitapreta
@fitapreta.vinhos

Listings

BEST OF THE REST

🐚 Nature at its Best

Parque Ecológico do Gameiro

Capped herons and kingfishers often fly through this ecological park in Mora. Follow the Passadiço do Gameiro, a walkway that begins at a small beach and continues along the riverfront, surrounded by wild country fields.

Passadiço do Alamal

About 60km from Portalegre, you'll find this pedestrian trail zigzagging along the river Tejo. Ducks and storks accompany you along the route overlooking the Castle of Belver.

Passadiços da Serra de Ossa

Crossing the valleys of Serra de Ossa, once a refuge for monks, these wooden walkways create a picturesque trail connecting the Aldeia da Serra to a small church on the outskirts of Redondo.

Parque Biológico da Cabeça Gorda

Thematic trails can be found inside this biological park near Beja. Deer are often spotted here as well as *silarcas*, wild mushrooms typical of the Alentejo.

Reserva Natural do Estuário do Sado

Amid the rice paddies of Alcácer do Sal and the dunes of the Troia beaches is this natural reserve home to dolphins and flamingos. Dolphin-watching trips depart from the Troia marina.

Reserva Natural das Lagoas de Santo André e da Sancha

Beaches and meadows surround these coastal lagoons where eels and waders are often spotted. Follow the Barbarroxa trail for a hike through the dunes or the Salgueiral da

Galiza, a picturesque route through oak trees and willow groves.

Parque Natural do Vale do Guadiana

The Guadiana river flows through this large natural park in the south of the Alentejo. Go for a swim along the margins of Mértola or hike from here to the dramatic waterfall of Pulo do Lobo.

🐴 Active Diversions

Coudelaria de Alter

This stud farm near Alter do Chão was created in 1748 to preserve the Lusitano horse breed. Visitors can join tours of the property and book horse-riding lessons.

Amieira Marina

Close to the village of Portel, this marina is the meeting point for sailing and fishing trips across the Alqueva Dam. Sleeping boats are also available.

Cocoon Portugal

Yoga retreats amid the Alentejo countryside are hosted regularly on this farm near Vila Nova de Milfontes.

Passadiço do Alamal

✖ Pork, Seafood & Slow Roasts

Alento €€

An old primary school turned into a seafood restaurant on the road to Praia das Furnas in Vila Nova de Milfontes. Fresh seafood is made to order and prepared on a wood-burning stove.

Taberna do Adro €

You'll find this cosy restaurant in Vila Fernando, on the outskirts of Elvas. Try the roasted chicken or pork and end with a slice of *sericaia*, a traditional egg pudding topped with plums.

Taberna Típica Quarta-feira €€

Forget the menu and trust the chef at this family-run tavern in Évora. Black pork is the star of the show here, just pick the wine and let the food parade begin. Bring cash.

Retiro do Ernesto €

From the sausage croquettes to the *caldo de beldroegas* (purslane soup with a poached egg), take your time savouring these local delicacies at this Moura restaurant.

Venda Azul €€

Generous portions and warm service draw visitors to this lively restaurant in the heart of Estremoz. Order the grilled black pork and don't leave without the courtesy shot of *ginjinha* or *abafado*.

Quinta do Quetzal €€€

Art, wine and food come together at this contemporary restaurant in Vidigueira. Enjoy a plate of slow-roasted lamb overlooking the vineyards.

Howard's Folly €€€

Don't stick to one dish, at Howard's it's all about sharing. Sirloin steak, langoustine rice or crispy shrimp are some of the dishes worth sampling along with a glass of Alentejo wine.

SERG ZASTAVKIN/SHUTTERSTOCK ©

Parque Natural do Vale do Guadiana

🍺 Craft Beers & Creative Cocktails

Cervejaria Sacarrabos €

Craft beers and sea views draw thirsty crowds to this local brewery in Sines. The perfect place to stop on your way to the beach or after a surf lesson.

Bar do Teatro Garcia de Resende €

Tapas and cocktails are on the menu at this small bar attached to a local theatre in Évora.

🛍 Picnic Fare & Handicrafts

O Cesto

Inside Évora's old town, on Rua 5 de Outubro, O Cesto sells a variety of handicrafts, such as cork bags, ceramic pots and wicker baskets.

Ar d'Alentejo Wines & Spirits

Wine, gin and liquor bottles cover the walls of this small shop in the village of Monsaraz.

Queijaria Bule

Sample delicious regional cheese at this local cheesemonger hidden within the white-washed walls of Serpa.

Scan to find more things to do in Alentejo online

THE ALGARVE

BEACHES | NATURE | SEAFOOD

**Experience
The Algarve
online**

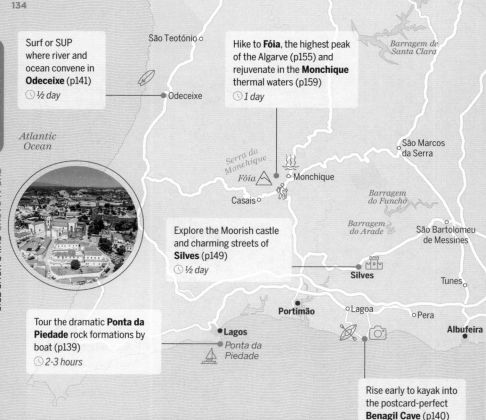

Surf or SUP where river and ocean convene in **Odeceixe** (p141)
🕐 ½ day

São Teotónio

Odeceixe

Hike to **Fóia**, the highest peak of the Algarve (p155) and rejuvenate in the **Monchique** thermal waters (p159)
🕐 1 day

Barragem de Santa Clara

Atlantic Ocean

Serra do Monchique

Fóia

Casais

Monchique

São Marcos da Serra

Barragem do Funcho

Barragem do Arade

São Bartolomeu de Messines

Explore the Moorish castle and charming streets of **Silves** (p149)
🕐 ½ day

Silves

Tunes

Portimão

Lagoa

Pera

Albufeira

Tour the dramatic **Ponta da Piedade** rock formations by boat (p139)
🕐 2-3 hours

Lagos

Ponta da Piedade

Rise early to kayak into the postcard-perfect **Benagil Cave** (p140)
🕐 2 hours

THE ALGARVE
Trip Builder

▬ Both an adventure playground and relaxing retreat, the Algarve promises coastal escapades, Atlantic swell, and epic hiking trails alongside beach bars, islands of golden sands, and thermal spa towns. Whitewashed villages, the freshest seafood and local *vinhos* complete the Algarvian experience.

Explore bookable experiences in The Algarve online

Experience traditions, creative workshops, history and heritage in **Loulé** (p149)
🕐 ½ day

Visit the fort at **Castro Marim**, followed by a natural salt-spa treatment (p159)
🕐 ½ day

Island-hop between sandbars in the wildlife-laden **Ria Formosa** (p156)
🕐 1 day

Traverse the charming streets, island beach, and castle ruins of pretty **Tavira** (p150)
🕐 1 day

Wine, dine and wander the old town, museums and marina of **Faro** (p151)
🕐 1 day

Parque Natural do Vale do Guadiana

SPAIN

Ameixial

ALGARVE

Serra do Caldeirão

Barranco do Velho

São Brás de Aportel

Loulé

Estói

São Jão da Venda

Faro

Olhão

Parque Natural da Ria Formosa

Reserva Natural do Sapal de Castro Marim e Vila Real de Santo António

Castro Marim

Vila Real de Santo António

Tavira

Atlantic Ocean

SOPOTNICKI/SHUTTERSTOCK ©
AMNAT30/SHUTTERSTOCK ©
JUAMPITER/GETTY IMAGES ©

N 0 _____ 20 km
   0 _____ 10 miles

Practicalities

PIERREOLIVIERCLEMENTMANTION/GETTY IMAGES ©

ARRIVING

Faro Airport Proximo buses connect the airport with Faro's bus and train stations (€2.35, 20 minutes), and EVA Transportes operate a three-times-per-day service to Albufeira, Portimão and Lagos. Visitors staying in resort towns can book group or private transfers in advance.

Coach & Train Lisbon trains connect to Tunes and Faro, where you can join the Algarve line. EVA and Rede Expressos long-distance coaches link the capital to the main Algarve hubs.

HOW MUCH FOR A

Small beer
€1.50

Cataplana for two €45

Parasol lounger rental €10

GETTING AROUND

Car hire Allows you the most freedom. Toll roads are easiest paid by an electronic transponder, usually issued with the rental, but can be avoided by using the slightly slower national highway.

Train Comboios de Portugal operates the Algarve train line – tickets and timetables online (cp. pt). Running at a leisurely pace between east and west, popular stops like Faro and Lagos have convenient stations. Other stops, such as Albufeira, are less central.

Buses EVA (eva-bus.com) link main towns regularly, with village schedules designed for commuters – weekends and holidays have minimal services. Local operators provide additional urban services, such as Proximo in Faro.

WHEN TO GO

JAN–MAR
Some seasonal shutdowns; great winter weather for Europe

APR–JUN
Quiet beaches for pre-season dips; wildflowers dot hiking trails

JUL–SEP
Soaring temps; big crowds; peak accommodation prices

OCT–DEC
Enjoyable climate, fantastic surf and plenty of birdwatching

EATING & DRINKING

Seafood Cuisine in the Algarve is unsurprisingly focused on delicious fresh fish. Mouthwatering local delicacies include the copper-pot served *cataplana*, a slow-cooked stew usually with *amêijoas* (clams).

Guia piri-piri chicken In the peaceful parish of Guia, known as Portugal's 'Capital of Barbecue Chicken', you'll find the famed hot-sauce marinaded *frango* (chicken) being chargrilled on nearly every corner. Restaurante Ramires is considered the dish's birthplace.

Must-try	Best dish
Santa Luzia Octopus (p145)	Cataplana (p145)

CONNECT & FIND YOUR WAY

Wi-fi is complimentary in most cafes, restaurants and hotels, with some towns offering free central hotspots. Data-only SIM cards are affordable and easy to purchase, including from Faro airport.

Navigation Main roads are well signposted – brown signs indicate attractions. Maps don't always highlight trails, but tourism offices supply directions for main routes. (cyclingwalkingalgarve.pt)

VAN LIFE

The Algarve is a fantastic destination to explore by campervan, but illegal camping is a growing issue. Find authorised campsites online (autocaravanalgarve.com).

WHERE TO STAY

The Algarve's accommodation is varied – from luxurious and expensive golf hotels to wallet-friendly all-inclusive resorts, hostels and *turismo rural* stays in the countryside.

Location	Atmosphere
Faro	Good central connections, varied price points – for most visitors it's more of a gateway than a destination.
Vilamoura	Home to the largest marina in Portugal, with high-end hotels, a casino, premium dining and bars.
Albufeira	Great nightlife, with a party 'strip' and historic old town. Hostels and all-inclusive resorts in abundance.
Lagos	Laid-back by day and lively by night. Accommodation for all budgets and types of traveller.
Monchique	Mountain retreat surrounded by nature, with health-focused resorts and thermal spas.
Costa Vicentina	Boutique rural tourism stays and ocean-side surf school retreats dot the west coast.

MONEY

Carry cash – smaller places often don't take cards. *Prato do dia* (dish of the day) and *vinho da casa* (house wine) are usually surprisingly decent and affordable away from the beachfront restaurants.

18

Caves, Bays &
BEACHES

KAYAKING | WALKS | FAMILY FUN

The deliciously diverse Algarve coastline, where vast swathes of soft golden sands meet dramatic caves and cliff-flanked coves, promises the perfect beach day out. Atlantic swells entice surfers to the west coast, families can unwind on Blue Flag beaches, and ocean adventurers will love kayaking into footprint-free bays.

How to

Getting around EVA buses visit most resort towns, and trains serve a few of the principal beaches. Arrive early to guarantee a parking space.

Accessibility The Algarve has 46 accessible beaches with varying facilities, such as access ramps, accessible toilets, and amphibious wheelchairs. A full list is available online (visitalgarve.pt).

Stay safe Erosion and currents are a threat. Avoid lounging under hanging rocks, keep away from cliff edges on trails, and try to swim at seasonal life-guarded beaches.

Pack Your Day Bag

Arm yourself with walking shoes, reef-friendly sunscreen and a sense of adventure to hop between beaches backed by jaw-dropping jagged cliffs, kayak into quieter bays and explore famous sea caves.

Lagos to Ponta da Piedade Towering sandstone cliffs and crystal-clear waters shape this famous point 3km out of town. Dreamy beaches garnish the walk, with **Praia dos Estudantes'** rocky tunnelled archways and the steep-staircase vistas of **Praia do Camilo** standouts. At the headland, descend the steps into a sheltered cove, where fishing boats depart on tours through surrounding caves. Adventurous souls can opt to explore **Ponta da Piedade** on a kayak tour, departing from **Fortaleza de Lagos**.

☼ Picturesque ≈ Pitch Ups

Settle in for the day at these long stretches of sands, with all the usual facilities. **Praia da Rocha** is home to NoSoloÁgua beach club, with striking rock formations to the west. **Falésia**, flanked by copper-hued cliffs, spans 6km from Vilamoura. **Meia Praia** in Lagos offers easy access by train to water sports.

Left Praia da Falésia **Above left** Praia da Marinha (p140) **Above right** Fortaleza de Lagos

Seven Hanging Valleys Trail Start early at award-winning **Praia da Marinha** before following the signed cliff route to **Benagil**, home to a poster-child cave, best accessed by kayak rental. The trail (6km one way) rises and falls between peaceful coves before officially ending at **Vale de Centeanes**. Continue to **Carvoeiro** (2km); a charming fishing village turned tourism hotspot, for the **Algar Seco** rock formations and plenty of restaurants.

Praia de São Rafael to Galé A mostly well-trodden yet sometimes challenging route (around 6km one way) links bays and beaches to the west of **Albufeira** together, with an occasional detour inland. Join a morning SUP tour of majestic cave tunnels and inaccessible bays (albufeirasurfsup.com) in **São Rafael** before following the tracks and resting your towel on whichever beach takes your fancy. Low tide promises natural swimming pools and reveals access to otherwise unreachable coves.

The Costa Vicentina

Windswept, rugged and less-visited, the west coast of the Algarve forms part of a nature park, linking the Algarve with the Alentejo. This refuge of birdwatching, surf adventures and boundless beaches provides a wilder contrast to the resorts on the south coast.

Stretching from **Burgau** to **Odeceixe**, there are plenty of near-deserted beaches to dig your feet into. Standouts include **Amoreira**, reaching inland along the Aljezur river, **Bordeira**, where sand dunes and surfers unite, and **Castelejo**, with the approach along the verdant hill road adding to its spectacle. It's easily experienced as a road trip: hop between scenic shores and dramatic viewpoints to appreciate every angle.

Left Praia da Bordeira Below Cacela Velha

Flip-Flop Friendly

Kick-back and relax on golden sands, coupled with easygoing walks, water sports or boat trips.

Odeceixe Surf the Atlantic and SUP in calm river waters all in one day at this breathtaking beach. **Praia das Adegas**, an adjoining sheltered cove, is an official naturist beach, while a detour over the Alentejo border will give you the best photos from the cliff-edge viewpoint.

Praia Grande, Ferragudo This traditional white-washed village retains all its charm, with fishing boats in the seafood-restaurant-lined harbour and a spacious beach under the shadow of an old castle. Take a break from bathing for a responsible marine-biologist-led boat trip to witness wild dolphins (wildwatch.pt).

Ilha de Faro Some of the Algarve's most serene beaches are on the islands in the **Ria Formosa** (p156), with regular public ferries, water taxis, and tour boats. Easily accessible by road bridge, residential Ilha do Faro is ideal for a lengthy walk along the sand-dune-backed beach. Continue across the Quinta do Lago Bridge to join the Ludo Trail, a flat walkway with panoramic mountain and island views, plus occasional flamingo sightings. Further east, **Cacela Velha**, with its charming fort village, and **Fuseta**, are magical at low tide when you can wade between sandbars.

19

Exploring the
COAST

ADRENALINE | OUTDOORS | UNDERWATER

Surf Atlantic waves, cross the coast by bike, discover shipwrecks or marvel at the shoreline with a bird's-eye view – the coastline of the Algarve is equally adrenaline-inducing as relaxing. For those with restless sandy feet, multi-day treks, coasteering adventures and underwater experiences will captivate – while jet-skiing, windsurfing and other water sports can be found in most resort towns.

🗺 How to

Getting around Many activity operators offer hotel pick-up for an additional charge.

When to go Water temperatures peak in August, around 23°C, falling to lows of approximately 15°C in winter. Some activities close in the low season.

Environment & safety
Protect the fauna and flora along the coast and stay safe on the cliff-top paths by following trail markers and directions. Always undertake extreme activities with a guide.

SERGIO SERGIO/SHUTTERSTOCK ©

Left Limestone cliffs and caves, Portimão **Far left top** Paraglider over Praia da Cordoama **Far left bottom** Hiker on the Rota Vicentina

Surfing Exhilarating Atlantic swell, retreats and schools make the Algarve an excellent address for both enthusiasts and learners. **Praia da Arrifana** is a year-round destination, with **Sagres** and **Lagos** both popular surf towns.

Scuba diving The Ocean Revival Project (oceanrevival.org) off the coast of **Portimão** consists of four Portuguese Navy vessels sunk to create an artificial reef. The remains of the B-24 Liberator Bomber in **Faro** and wreck-diving in **Sagres** present further unique underwater adventures.

Coasteering Experience an adrenaline-packed afternoon of cliff-jumping, climbing and swimming in sea caves between Sagres and Lagos. (coastlinealgarve.com)

Paragliding Fly high with a magical perspective above striking cliffs and beaches. **Praia da Cordoama**, on the windswept west coast, is one of the best places to take flight. Local guide Nelson Pacheco (flytripalgarve.webnode.pt) can advise on the most suitable spots.

Hiking Ramble between cliffs and bays on the **Fishermen's Trail**. The demanding 226km **Rota Vicentina** route links west-coast Algarve and the Alentejo on a remarkable 13-stage hike. Easily hop between rural accommodation, such as Aldeia da Pedralva, a reconstructed Algarvian village, using luggage transfer services (vicentinatransfers.pt).

Cycling From **Cabo de São Vicente**, mainland Portugal's most southwesterly point, to **Vila Real de Santo António** in the east, the 214km **Ecovia** is part of the EuroVelo, stretching from Sagres to Scandinavia. Bike paths and roads link the route, dipping between coastal views and inland towns.

✦ Coastal Conservation

The Algarve's limestone cliffs have been formed by numerous layers of marine fossils over 24 million years. Erosion has created stacks, arches and hidden caves – where small entrances lead to large grottos, illuminated by sunbeams through blowholes.

Sheltered water bodies, such as the Arade Estuary, act as nurseries to schools of juvenile fish. Swimming and snorkelling, rather than boat trips, minimise interference with ecosystems and allow sightings of colour-changing octopus, elusive cuttlefish, curious triggerfish and beautiful starfish.

Inês Nunes, a local marine biologist who founded Zip&Trip to help travellers responsibly explore caves and marine life around Alvor and Ferragudo. (zipandtripalgarve.com).

Taste the
OCEAN

SEAFOOD | CATAPLANA | MARKETS

▬▬▬ Straight-off-the-boat seafood and succulent crustaceans are dished up in *marisqueiras* across the coast. The region's cuisine is defined by fisherfolk, with some historical Moorish influences evident in dishes such as *cataplana* and Xerém stew. Grilled plates of sardines and octopus, alongside clams, oysters and cockles, complete the menu.

TRAVELVIEW/SHUTTERSTOCK ©

🗺 How to

Market visits Most towns sell fresh fish at their markets, with the most impressive in Loulé and Olhão. Hours are usually 7am until early afternoon, Monday to Saturday.

Rota do petiscos In October, sample numerous *petiscos* (small plates) and drink pairings from €3 at participating restaurants. (rotado petisco.com)

Fishy festivals Stalls of delicious seafood spread out across Olhão and Faro, ideal for tasting a bit of everything, on specific dates in July and August.

MAURO RODRIGUES/SHUTTERSTOCK ©

Left Polvo, Santa Luzia **Far left top** Loulé market **Far left bottom** Festival do Marisco, Olhão

Dishes Worth a Detour

Don't miss out on these Algarvian delicacies, best sampled in their honorary 'homes' with ocean views and a salty sea breeze.

Polvo in Santa Luzia The *esplanadas* of Santa Luzia are lined with restaurants all serving one speciality – **octopus** – and it's here, in the self-billed 'Capital of Octopus' you'll discover just how exceptional this dish can be. Extensive menus list various preparations of *polvo* – opt for it simply grilled, baked or boiled to appreciate the fresh flavours.

Sardinha Assada in Portimão Wafting from the harbour-side BBQs of Portimão, the scent of **grilled sardines** will tempt you before even seeing a restaurant. So celebrated are these salty morsels, the city hosts an annual Sardine Festival for a few days in early August, which has peaked at 100,000 people attending – though you can enjoy this tin-free treat any time.

Xerém de conquilhas in Olhão Many locales lay claim to this traditional Moorish-influenced **maize stew**. The recipe varies, though the cockles version of the dish was shortlisted in the top 21 Wonders of Portuguese Gastronomy.

The menu continues... Countless other seafood recipes adorn the menu with oysters, shellfish platters, and hand-harvested clams from the Ria Formosa excellent eats. Further specialities such as *caldeirada à algarvia,* a regional fish stew, and *arroz de tamboril,* monkfish rice, pair perfectly with a crisp Algarvian white wine.

Cataplana

An icon of the Algarve's gastronomy, a **seafood cataplana** for two is one meal you can't miss. The word *cataplana* itself refers to the clam-shaped metal pan, historically crafted from copper or brass, in which the ingredients are steamed slowly. With similarities to the tajines of Morocco, it's believed to date back to the Moorish period, when the Algarve was known as Al-Andalus.

The dish has many recipes, predominantly seafood-based, with clams or other crustaceans and fish as the stew's core ingredient. Find recipes, or even better, book a Faro **Cataplana Cooking Experience** on the dish's dedicated website. (cataplanalgarvia.pt)

ALGARVIAN
Traditions & Tastes

01 Cork
Cork harvesting continues in the Algarve. Learn more on a factory tour in São Brás de Alportel (eco-corkfactory.com).

02 Lighthouses
Testament to the nation's maritime history, lighthouses are littered across the coastline, with some open for visitors on Wednesday afternoons.

03 Frango da Guia (piri-piri)
The world-famous Algarvian staple. Chicken, charcoal-grilled, with a spicy chilli marinade or sauce, best experienced at Ramires in Guia.

04 Doce Fino do Algarve
Almonds are abundant in the region, and these colourful marzipan sweet treats are a delicious way to savour them.

05 Medronho
These red fruits distil into *aguardente* (a fire-water spirit). Visit Casa do Medronho in Marmelete (casadomedronho. com) for tours of local producers.

06 Pottery
Colourful ceramics and pottery adorn Algarvian walls and tables. Choose a souvenir and see traditional hand painting

at Porches Pottery
(porchespottery.com).

07 Corridinho do Algarve

This regional folk dance, performed in traditional outfitted pairs, sadly can only be spotted at rare festival performances these days.

08 Flor de Sal de Tavira

Used and celebrated in dishes and spa treatments, the *salinas* (salt pans) of Tavira are wonderful to walk through.

09 Wicker Baskets

Basket weaving is an age-old Algarvian tradition. Try palm weaving yourself at the Loulé Criativo workshops (loulecriativo.pt).

10 Oranges

Algarvian citrus fruits are renowned, and the sweet scent lingers inland. Pick up a fresh bag from a roadside stall.

11 Vinhos do Algarve

Fantastic wines, and vineyards, can be visited and tasted around the four wine regions of Lagos, Portimão, Lagoa and Tavira.

21 Stopping into
TOWN

CULTURE | HERITAGE | HISTORY

The Algarve's towns and villages reveal their secrets slowly. Narrow streets lead to medieval castles, traditional-craft workshops sit beyond ajar doorways, river sailings link fishing villages to inland towns, and an evening out could be Michelin dining or late-night hedonism – the choice is all yours.

🗺 How to

Getting around Most towns can be reached by EVA bus or train, and once there, are easily explored on foot. A car will make villages more accessible.

Museums & monuments Entry is affordable, often less than a few euros. Hours vary between seasons and weekends; calling ahead to check times is advisable.

Historic stays The Estói Palace, outside Faro, has been renovated as an attractive Pousada hotel.

Perfect Pairings

Mix and match historic towns and white-washed villages for a day trip of culture, nature and local experiences.

Ferragudo & Silves Get lost among the bougainvillea-framed streets of Ferragudo, a charming fishing village, complete with a grand beach and seafood-restaurant-lined harbour. Take the train to Silves (stations are a short walk), or if tides allow, book a boat tour up the Arade River (ferragudoboattrips. com). Explore the well-preserved castle and cathedral, and tour the narrow streets of the old Moorish capital. End the day with a tasting at a local vineyard (p161).

Loulé & Alte One of the largest inland towns, Loulé is awash with traditional craft workshops you can visit (loulecriativo.pt)

🛏 Digital Nomads

A small but growing scene, Lagos, with its laid-back coffee culture, is proving a popular destination for extended stays. Loulé and Faro are less touristy and more affordable alternatives – all three have co-working or shared office spaces. Since the pandemic, many hotels have started offering shorter 'workcation' packages.

Left Castelo de São João de Arade, Ferragudo **Above left** Ferragudo alleyway **Above right** Estói Palace

and impressive historical sights such as the castle and convent. Enjoy coffee in the art-deco Café Calcinha, and buy a picnic lunch from the art-nouveau market. Drive 25km to **Alte**, one of the Algarve's most authentic villages, and devour your dishes at the picturesque *fontes* (traditional water sources) before taking a dip in the **Queda do Vigário** waterfall.

Tavira & Cacela Velha The Rio Gilão, crossable by Roman bridge, links the two sides of this attractive town together. Marvel at panoramic views from the castle ruins or Camera Obscura, enjoy lunch river-side, or relax on the beach of Ilha de Tavira, accessible by boat. To the east, Cacela Velha is an enchantingly petite village, with a fort perched above a gorgeous beach.

A Brief Algarve History

Long before tourists, the Algarve had been settled and redefined throughout the ages. Some 3000 years ago, the Phoenicians were first, then the Carthaginians, followed by the Romans – remains of their period visible in Milreu and Cerro da Vila, Vilamoura.

The Moorish occupation (8th to 13th century) is most evident in the narrow Medina-style streets of Silves, the historic capital of the then-named Al-Andalus region. Following the Christian reconquest, Jewish quarters grew in Lagos and Faro before the Expulsion, while trade flourished in the Age of Discovery, both in goods and horrifically enslaved people (Lagos was home to the first European Slave Market), turning Portugal into a major colonial power.

São Marcos
o da Serra
o Ameixial

Fóia △ o Monchique   A L G A R V E

Alte o   o Barranco do Velho

● Silves   Cacela Velha

Portimão   o Loulé   Tavira ●

● Lagos   o Ferragudo   ● Albufeira   o Estói

Faro ●

*Parque Natural
da Ria Formosa*

*Atlantic
Ocean*

0 ———— 20 km
0 ———— 10 miles

Left Castelo, Silves (p149) **Below**
Bone chapel, Igreja de Nossa Senhora
do Carmo, Faro

Hotspots & Hubs

Faro Stroll the marina, cross the grand Arco da Vila, and wander the medieval walled Cidade Velha (old town) where the Sé (Cathedral) dominates the orange-tree-lined square. Elsewhere in the region's capital, museums and side-street cafes will keep you entertained – with the Igreja de Nossa Senhora do Carmo bone chapel a unique visit. On Ilha de Faro, the city's beach sits under the flight path. Inland, the Roman Ruins of Milreu are worth a detour, while Gusto, one of the regions six Michelin-starred restaurants, can be sampled in nearby Quinta do Lago.

Lagos Breathtaking beaches, dramatic rock forma-tions and surf lessons are the main draws to laid-back Lagos. The town centre invites you to explore 16th-century walls, forts and castles and admire the baroque decoration of Igreja de Santo António. Seafood restaurants, trendy cocktail bars and pumping parties will see you into the early hours.

Albufeira Party all night on the bar-clad strip (home to the Algarve's main LGBTIQ+ venue, Connection Bar), wine and dine in the modern marina, or get a glimpse of the fishing past in the old town. Restaurants, shops and beaches are usually bustling, but you can still get a culture fix at the Museu de Arte Sacra or Museu Municipal de Arqueologia.

22 Adventures
INLAND

HIKING | BIKING | FLYING

Sail up rivers straddling two Iberian nations, hike to mountainous peaks for vistas of land and sea, relish refreshing dips under tumbling waterfalls or satisfy your speed craving on a Formula One racetrack – the Algarve's interior is ripe for adventure.

How to

Getting around Public transport is limited in the Algarve's interior. Travelling on your own steam, or by car, is the way to go.

Birdwatching Serra do Caldeirão and Serra de Monchique provide sightings of eagles and northern goshawks.

Waterfalls Queda do Vigário in Alte and Pego do Inferno outside Tavira are worth an early-morning visit to avoid the crowds. Water can be limited in the driest months.

Adventures on Wheels

Algarve Motorsports Park Playing host to the Formula One in both 2020 and 2021, the demanding and exhilarating **Autódromo do Algarve** has been placed firmly on the map – and you can tackle the track yourself. Get behind the wheel of a four-cylinder engine, cling on to a racing pro sports motorcycle as the passenger, or opt for the slightly calmer go-kart track experience. (autodromodo algarve.com)

Mountain Biking & Road Cycling Not just for ramblers, the mammoth and challenging **Via Algarviana** can be completed in five one-day stages. Cycle through most of the inland Algarve's highlights, ending with a well-earned ocean dip on the beaches of **Sagres**. Technical details and maps can be found on

The Guadiana River

Voyage inland from **Vila Real de Santo António** along the Spanish border defining **Guadiana**. TransGuardiana tours include a return cruise, with time to explore the medieval castle and attractions of **Alcoutim**. On land, the multi-day 65km GR15 trail partly follows the river, taking in this lesser-visited but history-rich stretch.

Left Autodromo do Algarve **Above left** Pego do Inferno **Above right** Touring bicycles, Figueira

the trail's website (viaalgarviana.org). For cyclists who prefer a smoother ride, there are numerous road routes to tackle, ranging from flat and friendly to intense sports training. Maps and listings are provided by the tourism board (visitalgarve.pt).

Quad Bike Pick your trail and head off on a dusty adventure. Zoom past 12th-century Paderne Castle, whizz through fragrant orchards, make haste on river crossings or ascend to **Alte**, one of the most picturesque villages in the Algarve, riding these turbo-charged four-wheel vehicles (quad-ventura.com).

Adrenaline Without Driving Get your off-road kicks safely in the passenger seat on a four-wheel-drive safari departing from Albufeira. With the wind in your hair, leave the resort far behind to discover cork forests, firewater distilleries, and local flavours of homemade honey – with stops at waterfalls and historical monuments along the way. (alsafaritours.com)

🪁 Up in the Air

Hot-Air Balloon Admire panoramic views of the Algarve mountains and coast from your basket in the sky. (algarveballoons.com)

Spain to Portugal Zipline Cross both a border and timezone on this short and speedy zipline from Sanlúcar de Guadiana in Spain to Alcoutim in Portugal. Boats link with the pickup point (times in Spain are +1), and kayak rental in Alcoutim makes for a relaxing post-flying experience. (limitezero.com)

Portimão Aerodrome Tandem parachute jumps, scenic flights and aerobatic flight experiences take off from this small airport. At the time of writing, skydives were suspended. (airemotions.com)

Odeceixe • ALGARVE — Via Algarviana — Alcoutim ǒ

Fóia △ • Monchique — Rocha da Pena — • Cachopo

Autodromo do Algarve — Alte ° — • Barranco do Velho

Portimão • — • Silves

Lagos • — Albufeira • — ⌂ • Loulé — • Tavira

Sagres — Olhos de Água — Faro •

Parque Natural da Ria Formosa

Atlantic Ocean

Ⓝ 0 ▬▬▬▬ 20 km
0 ▬▬▬▬ 10 miles

FAR LEFT: SOPOTNICKI/SHUTTERSTOCK ©, LEFT: MAURO RODRIGUES/SHUTTERSTOCK ©

THE ALGARVE EXPERIENCES

Left Alcoutim, Portugal and Sanlúcar de Guadiana, Spain **Below** Fóia peak

Ground-Level Action

Hiking Traverse some of the 300km **Via Algarviana**, a mighty stretch of trails spanning the width of the Algarve. Taking in little-visited villages, lakes, orange groves, and both of the region's mountain ranges, the 14 linear sectors serve up something for everyone. One of the most popular day hikes crosses **Fóia**, the highest peak of the Algarve (902m) in Monchique, with a challenging secondary trail to the Barbelote Waterfall. For a half-day circular hike, head to **Rocha da Pena**, in the Serra do Caldeirão, a limestone outcrop renowned for birdwatching.

Underground Exploring Armed with a hardhat and torch, head more than 200m below at the **Loulé Rock Salt Mine** for a two-hour guided tour including ancient geologic formations. Tours depart four times each weekday. (techsalt.pt)

Horse Riding Equestrians and learners are in good hands at the **Albufeira Riding Centre**, offering one- to three-hour rides on the outskirts of Olhos de Água. (albufeiraridingcentre.com)

High Ropes & Paintball With four locations, including Lagos and Albufeira, climb and swing through the trees at **Parque Aventura**, picking the course difficulty based on your preference, or gather a group together for some forest-based paintball escapades. (parqueaventura.net)

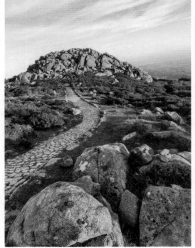

23 A Day Out in NATURE

ISLANDS | WILDLIFE | NATURE

▬▬▬ Pristine and protected, the expansive Parque Natural da Ria Formosa stretches some 60km along the coast. A labyrinth of barrier islands, salt pans, wetlands, marshes and dunes, it's a breathtaking destination for wildlife watching, island relaxing, seafood sampling, and nature-laden walks and trails.

THE ALGARVE EXPERIENCES

GONZALO AZUMENDI/GETTY IMAGES ©

🗺️ Trip Notes

Getting around Tours depart from various coastal towns. Public ferries to the islands are most easily accessed in Olhão; ticket sales open 30 minutes before departure. (etrioguadiana.pt)

When to go Ferry timetables run year-round to the inhabited islands, with winter best for birdwatching. The landscape can change drastically at low tide when local fishers hand-harvest clams.

Wildlife Beyond birds, the diverse ecosystem allows sightings of seahorses, chameleons, and the adorable Portuguese water dog.

🛏️ Overnight on the Islands

Limited accommodation options exist on the islands, including the Orbitur Bungalows on Armona. For a memorable getaway, spend a few summer nights on a private houseboat moored up alongside the islands. Fall asleep to the lapping waves, with a dinghy your gateway to the beach. (barcocasa.pt)

ALGARVE

05 End your day in nearby **Santa Luzia**, a fishing village famed for its *polvo* (octopus). It's served in various ways at the waterfront restaurants; **Casa do Polvo Tasquinha** is a favourite.

02 Skip the midday sun and head back to peek inside **Mercados de Olhão** before 1pm. Savour the catch of the day from one of the surrounding **seafood restaurants**.

● **Tavira**

Ilha de Tavira

Santa Luzia

03 Hire bikes, walk, or join a tour heading east through the **Quinta de Marim** salt pans for bird-spotting, or head west for a rejuvenating floating experience in the **Salinas do Grelha** (salinasdogrelha.pt).

Salinas do Grelha Olhão

Quinta de Marim

Ilha da Armona

Armona

Culatra

04 Drive to the **Praia do Barril** bridge, where a small train connects the island. Sip golden-hour cocktails overlooking the **Cemetery of Anchors**, a testament to the once-thriving tuna industry.

Ilha da Culatra

Farol

Parque Natural da Ria Formosa

01 From **Olhão**, take the early-morning ferry to the island's beaches. **Armona** is the closest, while **Culatra** and **Farol** are linked by a beautiful beach walk, with kayak rental available.

Atlantic Ocean

AMNAT30/SHUTTERSTOCK ©
SOPOTNICKI/SHUTTERSTOCK ©
RAPPHOLDT/SHUTTERSTOCK ©

N 0 _____ 10 km
   0 _____ 5 miles

Pamper, Unwind
& RELAX

YOGA | SPAS | NATURE

Fresh ocean air, orange-scented lands, and over 300 days of sunshine annually make the Algarve an ideal destination for a nature-fuelled wellness break. Pamper yourself with organic salt-spa treatments, unwind in hilltop thermal spa towns, or relax at multi-day antigravity yoga retreats. With a plethora of premium spas to choose from, it's simply a question of choosing your treatment.

M SWIET PRODUCTIONS/GETTY IMAGES ©

🗺 How to

Spa week Twice annually, for seven days (around March/April and October/November), some of the best spas in the region invite you to experience premium treatments and therapies with discounts of up to 50%. (algarve-spa-week.com)

Yoga You'll find drop-in classes in most major destinations, either in resorts or local gyms, though a solo early-morning beach session is equally enjoyable.

Municipal facilities Small selections of free outside workout equipment can often be found in town parks.

DPA PICTURE ALLIANCE/ALAMY STOCK PHOTO ©

Left Spring water, Monchique **Far left top** Lagos beach meditation **Far left bottom** Villa Termal Caldas de Monchique Spa Resort

Salt Treatments Castro Marim, a historic fort and castle village, is renowned for its **Flor do Sal**, and taking a dip at **Salino água mãe** is a memorable way to feel the health benefits. Float in salt pans, soothe your skin with saline clay, and exfoliate with salt flower – book ahead for massages. You'll also find similar floating experiences near Olhão.

Thalassotherapy utilises the therapeutic qualities of seawater to relax and re-energise. Enhance your ocean-side holiday at the exclusive **Vilalara Resort** in Porches, one of the most celebrated centres in Europe. Guest spa packages combine both traditional and Thalassotherapy treatments.

Premium Spas promise a peaceful escape, and with many in the region offering guest access, you aren't limited to just one. At the boutique **Bela Vista Hotel & Spa** overlooking Praia da Rocha, you'll find a serene relaxation area. A Turkish bath and plunge pool accompany treatments, some inspired by local products, such as almonds. The spa at **VILA VITA Parc Resort** in Porches draws inspiration from the locale, using natural rocks and Algarvian hues in the modern facilities, with holistic and signature treatments.

Retreats are flourishing across the Algarve, with wellness activities built into your stay. **Alamos Retreat** in Guia offers on-site Antigravity Yoga, **Monchique Resort & Spa** has daily all-inclusive health-focused activities, and **Karuna Retreat** is known for meditation and yoga.

♨ Caldas de Monchique

Flowing through the mountains of **Monchique**, healing thermal waters with a high-alkaline level of 9.5 pH naturally lend themselves to health therapies. This verdant spa town is a soothing place for any visitor to venture, with a shaded walk through the waterways of **Parque Fonte dos Amores** a true treasure.

Book ahead to indulge in water rituals, mud wraps, massages or a dip in the thermal pool, as non-guests can enjoy reservations for therapies. The **Villa Termal Caldas de Monchique Spa Resort** consists of four different hotels, and an overnight sojourn could be your ticket to serenity. (monchique termalresort.com)

Listings

BEST OF THE REST

⁙ Festivals & Celebrations

Feira Medieval de Silves

Once the capital of the ancient Kingdom of the Algarve, Silves steps back in time for a week in August. Costumes, jousting shows, traditional dishes, flame-throwing and plenty more bring the streets to life. Check dates on the municipal website. (cm-silves.pt)

Festival do Contrabando (Smugglers Festival)

For a few days in March, the town of Alcoutim, on the Guadiana river, celebrates the historic period of smuggling between Portugal and neighbouring Spain. With a floating bridge constructed across the river for the event, you can walk across the water border and savour the celebrations on both sides, with markets, crafts and historical re-enactments.

📖 History & Learning

Mercado de Escravos (Slave Market Museum)

On a dark day in 1444, Lagos opened the first market for the sale of enslaved Africans to Europeans; now, a small museum shares information from this time, although some feel it doesn't go far enough to highlight the suffering or atrocities during this period of Portugal's history.

Centro Histórico Judaico de Faro

The cemetery of the former Jewish community in Faro houses a tiny museum, with furniture and brief history notes of the former Faro synagogue. Found close to the football stadium.

ID Rota Vicentina

On the Algarve's west coast, and stretching into the Alentejo, the cultural program offered by the Rota Vicentina (a group of 200 local businesses) provides the chance to experience traditions such as engraving techniques and farmhouse stays. (rotavicentina.com)

Cerro da Vila

Moments from Vilamoura Marina, this small archaeological site of Roman ruins is the best-maintained in the Algarve. Walk the outside remains, and learn about the region's Roman history in the small exhibition.

Projecto TASA

Keeping ancestral craft techniques alive, TASA (projectotasa.com) in Loulé and Faro has boutique shops of local crafts and occasional workshops to learn skills first-hand.

👪 Family Fun

Aquashow

This large water and theme park promises plenty of entertainment inland from Vilamoura, including a 'water-coaster' and wave pool.

Golfland

The Algarve is renowned for its fantastic golf courses, and this tropical mini-golf in Alvor allows the kids to practice their putt too.

MAURO RODRIGUES/SHUTTERSTOCK ©

Festival do Contrabando, Alcoutim

FIESA Sand City

When sandcastles just aren't cutting it any more, head to FIESA, a large sand sculpture theme park just off the EN125 in Lagoa. Designs range from popular music stars to world-famous locations, and differ year to year.

Slide & Splash

One of the best waterparks in Portugal, this large, well-maintained land of slides and pools near Carvoeiro is a fun day out for all ages.

🍺 Vines & Brews

Morgado Do Quintao €€

Under the shade of a 2000-year-old tree just outside Silves, this family-run vineyard invites you to lunch at 'The Farmers Table'. Enjoy a selection of delicious local dishes and a flight of wine from the estate.

Quinta Dos Santos Tap House & Vineyard €€

Find this combined vineyard, craft brewery and trendy restaurant between Carvoeiro and Ferragudo. Taste wines and beers made on-site, alongside homemade dishes.

Algarve Rock Tap Room €

Not far from Faro Airport, this modern craft brewery makes the most of local ingredients. Swing by the Tap Room for a tasting, but check opening times in advance.

🍸 Beach Clubs & Bars

NoSoloÁgua Portimão €€

This trendy destination on Praia da Rocha has shoreside loungers, an ocean-facing pool, and musical beats accompanying the extensive cocktail and world-cuisine menu.

Thai Beach Vilamoura €€

Sip on expertly crafted cocktails and devour delicious Thai tasting menus to the backdrop of Praia da Falésia. This bar and lounge is a great lunch spot and equally renowned for its events and parties.

Vale do Lobo

Caniço €€

Built into the cliffs of Alvor and reached by an elevator in the rocks, this bar and restaurant's cove setting is spectacular. In summer months, late-night parties spill out onto the sand.

⛳ 18-Holes

Vale do Lobo

With two spectacular 18-hole championship golf courses close to Vilamoura, it's hard not to be distracted by the ocean views at Vale do Lobo, one of the premium golfing destinations in the Algarve.

Penina

On the outskirts of Portimao, the Algarve's first 18-hole course, and home to the Portuguese Open numerous times, the Sir Henry Cotton Championship Course makes for a great round.

Golf Societies

There are a range of Algarve golf societies that allow non-members to play. 6 Golfe, based at Vale de Milho, hosts games across the Algarve and guests can find and book upcoming rounds online (6golfealgarve.com).

 Scan to find more things to do in The Algarve online

25 The 12 Historic
VILLAGES

HISTORY | RUINS | CASTLES

███████ Lose yourself among schist homes hidden by nature, clamber up boulder-topped buildings for impeccable vistas, and marvel at age-old traditions and military forts among the 12 Aldeias Históricas de Portugal. Take a remote and rewarding journey into Portugal's past.

⌖ How to

Getting here Car rental provides easy access; however, a mix of bus (Rede Expressos and Transdev) and train journeys can get you to, or at least close to, most villages. Comboios de Portugal offers a summer train/bus day trip to Monsanto.

When to go Spring and Autumn have fewer crowds and comfortable hiking temperatures. From June to November, events take place as part of the '12 em Rede' festival.

The great hike For those with plenty of time, the Grand Route 22 links all 12 villages.

SIDE TRIP THE 12 HISTORIC VILLAGES

Amazing Aldeias

Make a beeline for these (highly subjective) stars of the show:

Monsanto Mesmerising panoramic views of rocky outcrops, parched pastures, and green mountains pierce the sky from Monsanto's prime position high on a hill. Here, boulders and buildings are as one – precariously floating above and between homes while doorways seemingly lead into giant stones. Tight streets of towers and churches, decorated with colourful plant pots, lead up to the Knights Templar castle. By sunset, devoid of day trippers, you'll be left in awe, wondering how this truly mystical place was awarded 'The Most Portuguese Village in Portugal' – when it's as far from typical as you can get!

≋ Why These Villages?

Located in the border region with Spain, these twelve villages played a crucial role in defending the nation – hence the prevalent fortifications and castles. The Aldeias Historicas program aims to preserve this heritage and bestowed the classification.

Learn more and plan your route at aldeiashistoricas deportugal.com.

Left Sortelha (p164) **Above left** Monsanto **Above right** Fortress gate, Castelo Rodrigo (p165)

Piódão Nestled in the lush green landscape of the Serra do Açor (Goshawk Mountains), the schist village of Piódão, unlike the others, is more known for housing fugitives than its role in the country's history. The narrow streets climbing the terrain are a delight to wander. Even more impressive when viewed from afar (especially illuminated at night), the whitewashed and blue-detailed church makes a striking contrast to the stone buildings and surrounding nature.

Sortelha Looking down from the 13th-century castle, Sortelha spills out in all its grand history. Alleyways of granite homes, Gothic gateways, medieval tombs, a renaissance church and a Manueline pillory combine to tell the history of one of Portugal's oldest towns – all wrapped up in magnificent walls and a landscape dotted with imposing granite boulders (look out for the Old Lady's Head, a huge boulder with an uncanny resemblance to a sharp-chinned witch).

🛏 City Stopovers

Accommodation options are available in most villages, making a road trip between them (stopping at two to four per day) an ideal choice – alternatively, the nearby cities can make good pit stops, detours or bases.

Guarda Located centrally to most villages, Guarda is the perfect multi-night base. Admire the cathedral's Gothic and Manueline architecture, stroll through the Old Jewish Quarter, and learn the region's history at Guarda Museum.

Castelo Branco When visiting Monsanto, stopping at Castelo Branco is a must to take in the Templar Castle ruins and views before touring the Baroque Bishop's Palace Gardens – the statued staircases are a spectacle.

Left Piódão **Below** Marialva

Discover All Dozen

Almeida, dating back to Roman times, houses military fortifications inside the star-shaped walls.

Belmonte's synagogue is a great starting point to learn about the town's Jewish history.

Castelo Mendo comprises two parts: the medieval citadel and the Dionysian walls of the Barbican.

Castelo Novo offers a striking location, set against the Serra da Gardunha mountains, granite houses, Templar fortifications, castles and churches.

Castelo Rodrigo is defined by medieval ruins and sights. The church, cistern and Cristóvão de Moura Palace are of particular interest.

Idanha-a-Velha is easily hiked to from Monsanto. The ancient streets and cathedral of various periods make this Roman sight a worthy visit.

Linhares da Beira is best admired from the skies. Gaze down on the 12th-century village at this popular paragliding spot.

Marialva takes on an almost mythical appearance when the clouds roll in. For a magical experience of the citadel, overnight at Casas do Côro (casas docoro.pt).

Trancoso, one of the largest villages, is best visited on a Friday for the weekly market – be sure to try the local sardine-shaped fried sweets!

PORTO

AUTHENTIC | ECLECTIC | HISTORIC

Experience
Porto online

PORTO
Trip Builder

Porto's profile rose quickly as a prime tourist destination and gateway to the north. The area offers activities for all types of travels, but exploration is best on foot as Portugal's second city is compact and dense with sights.

Explore bookable experiences in Porto online

Climb **Torre dos Clérigos** and attend a pipe organ concert (p179)
🕐 *1-3 hours*

View the impressive tiled interior of **São Bento Railway Station** (p175)
🕐 *1-2 hours*

Find a shady spot for a picnic with views in the **Jardim das Virtudes** (p183)
🕐 *2 hours*

Stop for refreshments in **Praça da Ribeira** after exploring the historic neighbourhood (p180)
🕐 *½ day*

Head across to the Gaia port lodges via the **Ponte Luís I** (p189)
🕐 *½-1 hour*

Practicalities

ARRIVING

Porto Airport is 30 minutes from the centre by direct metro.
Campanhã Station for intercity rail and terminus for *Alfa Pendular*.
Rodoviário (Campo 24 de Agosto) is the main coach terminal.

FIND YOUR WAY

Google Maps and other apps have integrated Porto's metro and bus network, which helps find stops and map out journeys.

MONEY

Look for ATMs with the white-and-blue 'Multibanco' logo for the best exchange rates. Carry cash for small merchants.

WHERE TO STAY

Location	Atmosphere
Foz & Matosinhos	Hotels and tourist apartments, some with ocean views
Boavista	Hotel chains are located in business district
Cedofeita, Sé, Miragaia, São Nicolau e Vitória, Santo Ildefonso	Boutique hotels offer ambience and proximity to monuments
Bonfim	Residential but still within walking distance to centre

EATING & DRINKING

Francesinha, the signature sandwich (pictured), originated in the 1950s from a Portuguese émigré.

Green wine (and red green wine), not just red and white wines. Pair with seafood.

Must-try
Sandes de pernil com queijo (pork loin sandwich with cheese) at Casa Guedes.

Best bifanas
Pork sandwiches with a bite at Porto's much-loved Conga restaurant (pictured left).

GETTING AROUND

Metro covers a large area from Póvoa de Varzim (north) to Vila Nova de Gaia (south).

Buses serve the entire metro area, but navigation can be confusing. Double-decker Bus 500 from the bottom of Aliados to the Mercado de Matosinhos is the one bus to take. Sit on the top deck on the left side for best viewing.

JAN–MAR	APR–JUN	JUL–SEP	OCT–DEC
Mix of rain and sun, may reach freezing overnight	May be rainy in April, mostly pleasant daytime temps	Summer temps 25°C to 30°C; tourist high season	Chilly overnight, daytime temps moderate, mix of sun and rain

26 Culinary QUESTS

HEARTY | UNPRETENTIOUS | DIVERSE

███████ Strike up a conversation with a Portuense about local food and be prepared for impassioned opinions on what you should try. We've prepared some suggestions for local dishes and drinks to sample, catering to both timid and adventurous palates.

AS FOOD STUDIO/SHUTTERSTOCK ©

🍴 How to

When to eat Restaurants close between lunch and dinner (3pm to 7pm or later). Head off your appetite with the Portuguese fourth meal of the day, called *lanche,* at a cafe/snack bar/*confeitaria* in the late afternoon.

What time For faster service, arrive at opening time when it's quieter and you can ask your server questions about your food without pressure.

Typical days of closure Sundays and Mondays.

MELISSA TSE/GETTY IMAGES ©

PORTO EXPERIENCES

Timid Palates

Bacalhau com natas Salted codfish is traditional Portuguese fare, although cod is not local. *Bacalhau com natas* is a rich mix with potatoes and cream – a gentler flavour that's difficult to get wrong. Pair it with a white wine *(vinho branco)* or green wine *(vinho verde;* p173). Try it at Adega Típica de São João (adegatipicasaojoao.negocio.site).

Pastéis de Chaves Originating in the northern city of Chaves, this flaky pastry has Protected Designation of Origin (PDO) status. Traditionally filled with minced veal, there are both savoury and sweet options, including chicken, vegetables, *bacalhau* and even chocolate. Find them at A Loja dos Pasteis de Chaves locations all over Porto. Pair the savouries with local craft beer.

Adventurous Palates

Lampreia A speciality from the northern river of Minho bordering Spain, the lamprey is a jawless vertebrate that looks like a creature from your worst childhood nightmare. When it's in season (January to April), lamprey is prepared either *à bordalesa* (Bordeaux style), or *à minhota* (Minho-style), which is a rice dish cooked with the lamprey's blood. Try it at Restaurante O Gaveto in Matosinhos (ogaveto.com) with *vinho verde tinto*, the 'red green wine'.

Tripas à moda do Porto A stew with veal tripe, white beans and *chouriço*. Try it out with a Douro red wine at Adega São Nicolau (facebook.com/AdegaSNicolau) in Ribeira or Líder (restaurante lider.com) in the northeast.

Left Typical Porto *confeitaria* **Far left top** *Bacalhau com natas* **Far left bottom** *Tripas à Moda do Porto*

✂ Local Specialities

Porto is rich in many wonders, and food and wine are two of the best things that our city has to offer. If you are looking for some kind of delicious 'fast food', there is one snack that you can't miss: *cachorrinhos* from Gazela. For octopus rice, the best place is Adega S Nicolau, where you can also eat a *quindim* for dessert. If you want to taste the typical *Tripas À Moda do Porto*, you should go to Líder. For wines, a Niepoort 87 and a Kopke are both always a good option.

Recommended by
Vasco Coelho Santos,
chef, Grupo Euskalduna,
euskaldunastudio.pt

What's on your table, Porto?

BRING A BIG APPETITE AND STRETCHY TROUSERS

Porto's gastronomy is influenced by its location at the intersection of the Atlantic Ocean, the Douro River, and the doorstep of the fertile Douro Valley. From traditional to modern, from catch-of-the-day seafood restaurants to fresh-from-the-oven bakeries, you will be well fed (and then some).

Left *Petiscos* **Middle** *Coxinhas de frango* **Right** *Pica-pau*

Petiscos & Other Savoury Bites

Petisco is the generic name for the Portuguese small dishes found at a variety of casual eateries such as *tascas* and *tabernas*, as well as cafes, *padarias*, *confeitarias* and snack bars. Remember: unlike Spanish tapas, *petiscos* are not free with drinks. Everything that arrives at the table is charged, including the basket of bread, butter, cheeses, patés, olives, and sometimes a large platter of petiscos. Don't be shy about sending back what you don't intend to consume, or it will show up on your bill and go to waste.

Trying to figure out what the fillings are by sight is mostly guesswork, but the upside is that the smaller sizes of *petiscos* let you sample an assortment of savoury bites:

Bacalhau *Bolinhos de bacalhau, pastéis de bacalhau, pataniscas de bacalhau, Iscas de bacalhau* (various shapes of salted cod, combined with other ingredients such as potatoes, flour and parsley)

Chicken *Coxinhas de frango, rissóis de frango* (rissoles), *empadas de frango* (small pies), *moelas* (gizzards)

Pork *Croquetes, bifanas* (sandwiches with pork marinated in white wine and garlic), *sandes de pernil com queijo* (sandwiches with pork shank and cheese)

Beef *Pica-pau* (translated to 'woodpecker'; beef pieces in a light gravy made with beer), *picanha* (rump steak)

Chouriço assado (sausage flambéed in a ceramic dish, served with bread), *chamuças* (Portuguese samosas), *tremoços* (lupini beans) and *bolo de carne* (sausage baked in bread) are also typical fare.

At the upscale end, seafood restaurants next to the commercial fish market in Matosinhos specialise in share plates such as *amêijoas à vulhão pato* (clams), *mexilhões* (mussels with white wine and garlic), *percebes* (gooseneck barnacles), *sapateira recheada* (stuffed crab), and classic *petiscos* such as *rissóis de camarão* (shrimp rissoles).

> Trying to figure out what the fillings are by sight is mostly guesswork, but the upside is that the smaller sizes of *petiscos* let you sample an assortment.

Vegan Options

Vegans, don't despair – you have options in Porto. The Portuguese kitchen is very meat- and fish-heavy, but the number of vegan restaurants is growing. Newer casual spots like Kind Kitchen, and combo cat rescue, coffeeshop and restaurant O Porto dos Gatos join mainstays such as Casa da Horta, a cultural and ecological association. Alongside these options, the DaTerra group of restaurants are now billed as vegetarian but many of the franchises are now 100% vegan.

Vinho Verde

There's more to the north than red and white wines, there's also 'green wine', which is not literally green, but a young wine that is only months old. There is also 'red green wine' *(vinho verde tinto)*, and a rosé version. *Vinho verde* is a Protected Designation of Origin (PDO) product from a geographical area inland from Porto, between the Minho and Douro rivers. Chilled, light and slightly fizzy, it's wonderfully refreshing on a hot summer's day.

✕✓ A Very Big Bite

You might have heard of Porto's gut-busting sandwich that is the *francesinha*. Its creation was inspired by the *croque monsieur* in France, but a *francesinha* is in a calorific league of its own. It has typically four or five types of meat layered between the bread slices, all of which is covered by cheese that's melted by the beer and tomato sauce, topped with a fried egg and served with French fries. This beast of a sandwich tends to intimidate the uninitiated but don't worry, even the locals are polarised on the 'love it or hate it' scale. You'll need an open mind, a big appetite, and a cold beer to tackle one.

27 Structures & **STYLES**

HISTORIC | MODERN | PRITZKER

▬▬ Porto is an ancient city, its historic centre a living museum of architectural styles from Portuguese Romanesque to contemporary. Across the passages of time, the city was largely spared from the devastating effects of natural disasters and WWII bombs, while centuries of artisans added their distinct layers to its facades.

🗺 **How to**

Getting around
Porto's historic centre is compact and walkable, if at times quite steep, with daunting staircases. Bring your sturdiest shoes.

Costs There are no fees to enter churches except for São Francisco, now only a museum. There is a small fee for the cloisters and museum of the Sé.

Best timing For the most popular monuments visit either at opening or closing time to avoid the tourist buses.

ARCHITECT ALVARO SIZA - EPHST/SHUTTERSTOCK ©

Left Faculty of Architecture building **Far left top** Igreja de Santa Clara **Far left bottom** Torre dos Clérigos

Medieval monuments Most of Porto's preserved monuments from the early Middle Ages lie within the Unesco area, although each has been restored and adapted multiple times. From the top of the hills down: the Sé, Medieval Tower and sections of the wall, the churches of Santa Clara and São Francisco. Igreja de São Martinho de Cedofeita, the oldest church in Porto, is outside the Unesco area and is suggested to be even older than recorded (11th century).

Baroque monuments Italian artist Nicolas Nasoni's baroque style is represented in Porto's most famous landmarks: Igreja (and Torre) dos Clérigos, Paço Episcopal, the facade of Igreja da Misericórdia, Palácio Do Freixo, the stonework of Igreja do Carmo and engravings in Igreja de Santo Ildefonso. His gilt carvings in the churches of Santa Clara and São Francisco, along with Ordem do Terço's exterior, are impressive.

Neoclassical monuments Renewal in the late 18th century led to some of Porto's most majestic buildings: Igreja da Lapa, Palácio das Carrancas (now Soares dos Reis Museum), Igreja Nossa Senhora da Vitória, Palácio da Bolsa, Alfândega do Porto and the neo-Palladian British Association building. During the 18th century Praça da Ribeira, originating in medieval times, was transformed to its current style.

Tile monuments Porto is famous for its decorative tiles called azulejos, adorning interiors and exteriors. Large-scale works can be found at: Capela das Almas, São Bento Railway Station, *Ribeira Negra* (panel), the churches of Santo Ildefonso, Carmo and Misericórdia, and outside the Sé.

⊘ Porto's Pritzker Prize Winners

The Pritzker Prize, architecture's annual international award to honour significant achievement, has been presented twice to alumni of the University of Porto: Álvaro Siza Vieira in 1992 and Eduardo Souto de Mora in 2011. Both are modernist architects who've gained international recognition for designs that harmonise with natural surroundings. Examples include Siza Viera's natural pools in Leça da Palmeira (1966), filled by ocean tides, and Mora's design of Braga Stadium (2004), melding into an old rock quarry. Álvaro Siza Vieira built the University of Porto's Faculty of Architecture building (1988–1992), integrating it with the cliff.

INSPIRED
By Devotion

01 Capela do Senhor da Pedra (1686)

Hexagonal church built on a rock on the beach, originally a site of ancient pagan worship.

02 Mosteiro da Serra do Pilar (1672)

Circular church and cloister design unique in Portugal; replica of Church of Santa Maria Redonda in Rome.

03 Igreja do Mirante (1877)

The oldest Protestant church in Porto, covered in decorative tiles designed by a church member, Delfim Gonçalves Vieira, in 1934.

04 Igrejas do Carmo e das Carmelitas

Two churches, Igreja dos Carmelitas (1628) and Igreja do Carmo (1768), separated by a 1m house.

05 Kadoorie Mekor Haim Synagogue (1938)

Synagogue and museum of the Jewish community of Porto, the largest synagogue in the Iberian Peninsula.

06 Igreja dos Clérigos (1750)

Baroque church with 75.6m bell tower, designed by Nicolas Nasoni, who is buried in the church's crypt.

07 Igreja de Nossa Senhora da Conceição (Igreja do Marquês; 1947)

Asymmetrical church with both Romanesque and Gothic architecture and grand views from the 50m tower.

08 Igreja de São Martinho de Cedofeita (1087)

Oldest church in Porto; rare example of a single-nave vaulted-ceiling temple.

09 Igreja da Lapa (1755, finished 1863)

Rococo and neoclassical, where the heart of King Pedro IV has been kept since 1835.

10 Capela Nossa Senhora da Silva (15th century)

Hidden Baroque chapel, the only one in Porto on the 1st floor, at Rua dos Caldeireiros 104.

11 Igreja de Santo Ildefonso (1739)

Covered by 11,000 tiles by artist Jorge Colaço in 1932, depicting biblical imagery and scenes from St Ildefonso's life.

12 Sé do Porto

Porto's cathedral dates to the 12th and 13th centuries, with a Roman-Gothic structure; some renovations were made in the Baroque period.

28 Porto from **ABOVE**

CLIMB | VIEWS | WALK

A bird's-eye view over the city of Porto is possible, depending on your preferred angles and what you'd like to see. Here are several novelty options, each around one hour and similar in price, but with different levels of vertigo and views, plus a few free options.

🗺 How to

Locations The novelty experience closest to the centre is Porto 360 located in the Crystal Palace Gardens, followed by the Ponte da Arrábida climb (a stop on the 500 Bus or short taxi ride), Serralves

for the Treetop Walk (Bus 203, Castelo do Queijo), then the lighthouse in Leça da Palmeira (20 minutes by taxi).

A moving panoramic view Take a ride in the Gaia Cable Car (gaia cablecar.com).

PORTO EXPERIENCES

Ponte da Arrábida Climb (opened 2016: 262 steps, 65m, €16 to €17.50, 40 minutes) At one time the largest concrete arch in the world, the Arrábida Bridge was completed in 1963 and is the last bridge on the Douro River before the ocean. Climbers ascend the arch towards sunset, taking in the views on either side, wearing safety equipment consisting of a harness and lifeline. (portobridgeclimb.com)

Parque de Serralves Treetop Walk (opened 2019: 260m of walkway, 1.5m to 15m in height, park ticket €12) The tree canopy provides a peaceful respite in the middle of urban Porto and an opportunity to observe the biodiversity of the park. One-hour guided tours are provided in Portuguese, French and English, and there are 90-minute family workshops on weekends. (serralves.pt/en/institucional-serralves/treetop-walk)

Porto 360 (opened 2021: 150 steps, €12.50, 40 minutes) Guided tours of the dome of the Super Bock Arena start with a history of the building from 1852 to the present day, then climb 150 stairs to the top of the dome to enjoy 360-degree views of the city. (superbockarena.pt/visitar/porto-360)

Monument(al) views If your thighs can stand it, we can also recommend: Torre dos Clérigos (75m, 240 steps, tower and museum €6, night pass €5); the much easier (and free) view from the Portuguese Centre of Photography; or the balcony of the Mosteiro de Serra do Pilar across the river (also free), part of the Unesco World Heritage site that includes Ribeira and the Ponte Luís I.

Left Views from Torre dos Clérigos **Far left top** Gaia Cable Car **Far left bottom** Parque de Serralves Treetop Walk

🗼 Climb a Lighthouse

A bit further afield, the most expansive view to be had is from the **Farol de Leça** (1926; amn.pt/DF/Paginas/FaroldeLeca.aspx), aka Boa Nova Lighthouse, in Leça da Palmeira, Matosinhos. At 46m, it is one of the tallest in Portugal, with a range of more than 50km of visibility on a clear day. Managed by the Maritime Police, the lighthouse can be visited for free (maximum six per group) from 2pm to 5pm Wednesdays, and 10am to 12.30pm on the first and third Sundays of the month.

29 Stroll through History
IN RIBEIRA

HISTORY | ART | PEOPLE

A Unesco World Heritage site since 1996, Ribeira is one of Porto's oldest neighbourhoods, its narrow streets and ancient walls lining the bank of the Douro River. Today it's bustling with street performers, restaurants and bars, marine activity, and pedestrians soaking up the lively atmosphere.

GAIL AGUIAR ©

🗺 Trip Notes

Getting around Ribeira is best explored on foot; some streets are very narrow and fill up easily.

Festivals & events Occasionally, major events shut down Ribeira, such as bike races, mass runs, and the biggest annual event, Festa de São João, on the eve of 23 June.

Peak months Visitor numbers are especially high during July and August; crowds thin in spring and autumn, while the atmosphere remains lively.

🚶 Descent to the Douro

As parts of the embankment have steep inclines, the walk will start at the high point beside the top bridge deck and make a descent to the river by stairs to save legs and lungs. If a cardio workout is desired, you may wish to do the itinerary in reverse.

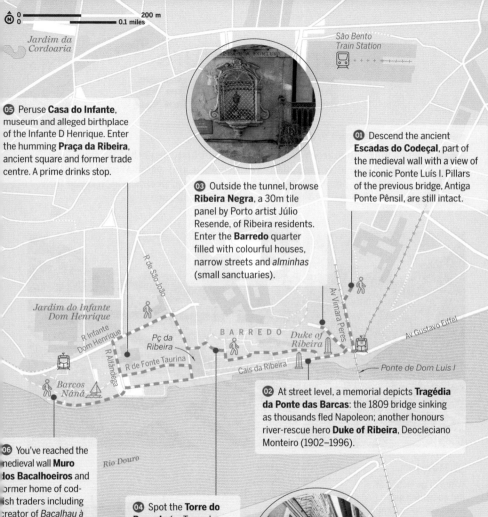

Jardim da Cordoaria

São Bento Train Station

05 Peruse **Casa do Infante**, museum and alleged birthplace of the Infante D Henrique. Enter the humming **Praça da Ribeira**, ancient square and former trade centre. A prime drinks stop.

01 Descend the ancient **Escadas do Codeçal**, part of the medieval wall with a view of the iconic Ponte Luís I. Pillars of the previous bridge, Antiga Ponte Pênsil, are still intact.

03 Outside the tunnel, browse **Ribeira Negra**, a 30m tile panel by Porto artist Júlio Resende, of Ribeira residents. Enter the **Barredo** quarter filled with colourful houses, narrow streets and *alminhas* (small sanctuaries).

Jardim do Infante Dom Henrique

R de São João

R Infante Dom Henrique

R Alfândega

Pç da Ribeira

R de Fonte Taurina

B A R R E D O

Duke of Ribeira

Av Vinara Peres

Av Gustavo Eiffel

Cais da Ribeira

Ponte de Dom Luís I

Barcos Nâná

02 At street level, a memorial depicts **Tragédia da Ponte das Barcas**: the 1809 bridge sinking as thousands fled Napoleon; another honours river-rescue hero **Duke of Ribeira**, Deocleciano Monteiro (1902–1996).

Rio Douro

06 You've reached the medieval wall **Muro dos Bacalhoeiros** and former home of cod-fish traders including creator of *Bacalhau à Gomes de Sá*; spot the **Barcos Nâná** model boats made by local character Fernando Teixeira.

04 Spot the **Torre do Barredo** (or Torre da Rua de Baixo) medieval civil architecture structure; note the flood markers recording the Douro River's major flooding events.

30 Urban Nature
ESCAPES

RELAXING | RECREATION | VIEWS

■■■■ Porto's municipal greens are a collection of historic gathering spots and modern landscape architecture, many with views to the water. Whether you're looking for a place to picnic, stretch out under the sun, people-watch or go for a walk, there's a park nearby to reconnect with urban nature.

SARJ3P/SHUTTERSTOCK ©

🗺 How to

When to go Note that the walled and gated municipal parks have different closing times during the year, but typically close by sunset every day.

Events & markets
Municipal parks often host events, plus weekend and seasonal markets for handicrafts, secondhand goods, food and specialty items. (porto.pt/en/articles/category/culture).

Tip The only public toilets within any of the municipal parks in the historic centre are in Jardins do Palácio Cristal.

WIRESTOCK CREATORS/SHUTTERSTOCK ©

MICHAEL YK CHO/SHUTTERSTOCK ©

Historic Parks in the Centre

Jardim das Virtudes Formerly the Porto Gardens Company, its terraces give a 3D effect and sense of seclusion and privacy. It has great views to Alfândega do Porto (Customs House), the river and Vila Nova de Gaia.

Jardins do Palácio Cristal Designed when the original Palácio de Cristal existed (19th century); peacocks wander freely. The park's municipal buildings include the Super Bock Arena – Pavilhão Rosa Mota, Museu Romântico, an acoustic shell and Almeida Garrett Municipal Library.

Jardim Marques de Oliveira Known locally as the garden of São Lázaro, it was Porto's first public garden in 1834. Built in a typical romantic garden style, it's great for people-watching.

Jardim de João Chagas Known locally as Cordoaria, from the days of rope-makers in residence from the 15th century. Another great location for people-watching; Tram 22 runs through it.

Further Afield

Jardim Botânico Created in 1951, it was the former residence of the family of Portuguese writer Sophia de Mello Breyner Andresen. It's now part of the Museum of Natural History and University of Porto.

Parque da Cidade The largest urban park in Portugal (83 hectares), with restaurants, sports facilities, ponds, a museum and an event venue. Finalised in 2002, there are already plans for expansion. There's a metro station nearby, making Matosinhos Beach fully accessible to wheelchair users using the metro network.

Left Jardim das Oliveiras **Far left top** Jardins do Palácio Cristal **Far left bottom** Jardim Botânico

🌱 Jardim das Oliveiras

Opened in November 2013, Jardim das Oliveiras is both a green roof and park to replace Praça de Lisboa. With 4500 sq metres of grass and 50 olive trees, it is a perfect chill spot in this busy quarter, in view of Torre dos Clérigos, Lello Bookstore, Rectory and Natural History Museum of the University of Porto. There is a bar and outdoor lounge as an alternative to the grass.

31 Port Wine **LODGES**

WINE | VITICULTURE | HOSPITALITY

■■■■ Looking for port wine lodges in Porto? Called *caves* in Portuguese, they're located on the opposite riverbank, in Vila Nova de Gaia. Port society names such as Warre's, Taylor's, Sandeman, Ferreira, and Graham's loom large over the warehouses and tasting rooms. The newest visitor centre is the World of Wine.

JAVARMAN/SHUTTERSTOCK ©

🗺 How to

Where to go Avoid crowds by visiting lodges further away from the river, as the closer ones are often included in packages with bridge cruise tickets.

Advance bookings If you are short on time or are part of a group, book a visit in advance.

Premium experiences
If your port wine knowledge is advanced, skip the tour and upgrade your tastings for a premium experience.

BENNY MARTY/SHUTTERSTOCK ©

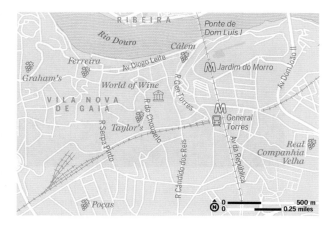

Tours & Tastings

Ever taken a port wine tour before? Be spontaneous and join the first tour with space. Guides will explain how port is made, why the Douro is a demarcated region, and why the cellars are in Gaia instead of Porto. You'll learn something about port, the city and Portugal's history at the same time. Tours are typically 20 to 30 minutes in the cellars on a regular schedule during the day.

Many lodges have generations of winemaking in their families and those stories can end up being the most fascinating part of the tour. Visits usually end in a tasting room and shop, where the guide will either commence an included port wine tasting or give you a menu to make your wine selection. If you're buying port as a present, you'll probably want to extend your tasting – all in the name of research, of course.

If you are still undecided about which port lodge to visit, here are some for consideration: **Ferreira** offers the opportunity to learn about Dona Antónia Adelaide Ferreira, a powerful Portuguese businesswoman in a male-dominated industry; **Calém** ticket options include a fado show and (upcoming) 5D film; **Graham's** is a tastings favourite and has one of the best views; **Real Companhia Velha** is the oldest wine company in Portugal (265 years); **Poças** is a notable smaller producer owned and operated by a Portuguese family.

Far left top Graham's tasting room
Far left bottom Ferreira cellar

ⓘ Taylor's Visitor Centre

Taylor's revamped their visitor centre in 2017 to a self-guided, exhibition-style space. Audio guides are provided in 12 languages with one to two hours of information, plus 30 minutes for the tasting of two ports. Information is formatted for a spectrum of wine knowledge, from novice to aficionado, with no reservations required.

BARMALINI/SHUTTERSTOCK ©

Port: A Fortified Nectar

AN OLD DRINK FOR A NEW WORLD

Four centuries of historical association with British merchants has given traditional port wine a reputation for being an older-generation tipple. But in modern times, port wine producers are diversifying their product lines and targeting a wider audience and younger demographic. Part of this includes integrating into the food scene and, more recently, cocktails.

Left Douro Valley vineyard **Middle** Port tasting, Vila Nova de Gaia **Right** Grapes on the vine

Port has been linked to the city of Porto for centuries, ever since the first port shipping company was founded in 1638 by German ambassador Cristiano Kopke. The Marquês de Pombal established the Douro Valley wine region in 1756, making it one of the oldest demarcated appellations in the world. As a protected area, the name port can only be used for fortified wine that is produced in the Douro Valley wine region, with quality control by the IVDP (Instituto dos Vinhos do Douro e Porto). This regulation is important to an industry which accounts for a fifth of Portugal's export revenues.

Grapes & Types

Most port types come from six main grape varieties, but around 30 different grapes can be used to make port.

Ruby port could be called the 'gateway port' as it's mass-produced and inexpensive. The youngest of the traditional ports (three to five years old), it's simple, fruity, and commonly used in cooking. Try it in poached pears, or after dinner with chocolate truffles or sheep's cheese.

Tawny port is the most popular after-dinner port wine in Portugal. It's aged in wooden casks for at least seven years, which gives its colour, name, and a particular flavour profile in the ageing process through oxidation. Tawny Port can be consumed before dinner as an aperitif, with cheese and nuts during dinner, or accompanying a dessert.

White port is produced like a tawny, ageing for a year in oak tanks before moving to oak casks. Styles range from very dry to very sweet (*Lágrima* is the sweetest); it's consumed as an aperitif or dessert wine.

Recently, white port has grown in demand as the main ingredient in Porto Tónico, marketed as a light summer drink (5% alcohol), a refreshing cocktail of white port mixed with tonic water and lemon.

Rosé port – or pink port – is a relatively new lighter style. It's a young, fruity port typically aged a few years, best served chilled. Try it with strawberries and chocolate.

> As a protected area, the name port can only be used for fortified wine that is produced in the Douro Valley wine region.

Port in Food

Recipes can be a closely guarded secret in Porto, but port wine is a common ingredient in *francesinha* sauce. Some well-known places use port wine as an ingredient in their glazes and syrups, as is the case for Padaria Ribeiro's croissants.

While fruit-in-port desserts have been around for some time, such as *Pera bêbeda* (drunken pears) and *Maçã assada com vinho do Porto* (roasted apples), specialty products such as onion and port wine jam have become more mainstream. The very rich, sweet traditional dessert that is *Pudim de Abade de Priscos* also utilises port wine.

Port wine appears in many Christmas recipes, such as bread puddings *(mexidos* or *formigos),* cakes *(bolo-rei),* pastries in syrup *(sonhos com calda de vinho do Porto, rabanadas)* or without syrup *(bolinhos de jerimu),* and eggnog *(gemada com vinho do Porto).* Other local desserts using port wine such as 'dry soup' *(sopa seca)* are also seasonal, enjoyed at Carnaval and saints' festivals.

32 Waterfront **BIKE RIDE**

SCENIC | CYCLE | WATERFRONT

■■■■ Hire a bike and take a waterfront ride that you can enjoy at any pace – it's flat. Cruise along the river to the ocean, stopping at museums, forts, bridges and Porto's maritime waypoints. Freely explore and stop along the way.

IAN CUMMING/GETTY IMAGES ©

🗺️ Trip Notes

Bike hire Hire a bike in Matosinhos Sul (the end point) or in Porto centre near a metro station.

Metro card Buy a reloadable card to take your bike to the starting point (Campanhã metro station is the closest to Palácio do Freixo).

Start times Head off in the morning on shorter days, or after lunch on long summer days.

⛴️ Best of Both Worlds

Climb aboard the wooden *Menino do Douro* ferry boat for picturesque views of both sides of the river, where the Douro meets the ocean. Shut off the modern world for the 20-minute crossing as the car traffic and shoreline bustle fades away, taken over by lapping waves, creaking floorboards and squawking seagulls.

05 Cross under the **Ponte da Arrábida** (p179). Fill up on freshly grilled fish in scenic **Afurada**, which still retains its fishing village character.

03 The fifth bridge, Ponte de Dom Luís I (1886; pictured left), is a landmark of the city. Hop off the bike for a drink in historic **Ribeira** (p180), animated by street performers and tourists.

01 Start the journey at baroque **Palácio do Freixo**, stopping at 19th-century mills on one side and the National Press Museum on the other.

Campanha

Ponte da Arrábida

Rio Douro

São Bento

RIBEIRA

Estaleiro do Rabelo

Ponte de Dom Luís I

Ponte Maria Pia

Museu Nacional da Imprensa (National Press Museum)

Rio Douro

·URADA

Convento de Corpus Christi

General Torres

VILA NOVA DE GAIA

04 Cross the lower bridge deck to lively **Cais de Gaia**, home to the port lodges (p184). Mount up again, passing Convento de Corpus Christi (1345) and Estaleiro do Rabelo, the only shipyard that still makes *rabelo* boats.

02 Follow the river, passing the wrought-iron **Ponte Maria Pia**, the original railway bridge attributed to Gustave Eiffel, since replaced by the São Jõao Bridge (1991).

N 0 ——————— 1 km
0 ——————— 0.5 miles

Listings

BEST OF THE REST

🍸 Top Sundowner Spots

Aduela €

Popular tavern next to Carlos Alberto Theatre in the city's bar district, serving traditional Portuguese tavern snacks in a relaxed environment. The interior is small; most patrons sit outside.

Letraria Craft Beer Garden €

Hidden beer garden in Porto near Bolhão Market, with more than 100 different beers and 20 on tap. It has a kitchen and serves menu items to pair with the beer.

Capela Incomum €

Wine bar named 'Uncommon Chapel' in a 16th-century chapel (altar intact). Discover and taste a wide range of Portuguese wines, with staff sharing the story behind the wine.

Guindalense Futebol Clube €

Major points if you can find the entrance along a staircase (you'll pass by if taking the Funicular dos Guindais). Simple, with great views; a Porto classic sports bar.

Golden Oldie €€

For cocktails in a historic setting: the theme is Roaring '20s, cosy and classy with Charleston music, foxtrot and jazz. Located near Hospital Santo António and the University Rectory building.

Bonaparte Pub €

Irish-style sports pub filled with antiques and '80s music, it has a relaxing atmosphere with attentive bar staff. Wide selection of drinks at reasonable prices. Two locations (Foz and Porto downtown).

Mirajazz €

Local wines and live jazz music with incredible views of the Douro River, located in Miragaia. A bit hard to find – climb the staircase across from the Alfândega parking lot.

Terrace Lounge 360 – Porto Cruz €€

Fantastic rooftop lounge with grand views of Porto, in the middle of Caisa de Gaia. Porto Cruz is a port producer hosting events in its building, Espaço Porto Cruz.

Dick's Bar – Yeatman Hotel €€€

Outstanding views of Porto and the Douro River. Upscale service that is expected of the Yeatman Hotel, a property of Taylor's. Exceptional drinks selection in a convivial atmosphere.

🥖 Epicurean Picnic Delights

Comer e Chorar por Mais €€

More than a century old, the aptly named 'Eat and Cry For More' is a well-known Porto delicatessen carrying regional products from around Portugal. Knowledgeable and friendly staff; tastings possible.

Comer e Chorar por Mais

Garrafeira do Carmo €€

Specialty shop with a varied inventory of all types of spirits, domestic and imported; a wide variety of Portuguese wines with particular focus on port wine knowledge.

Casa Natal €

Established in 1900, this traditional delicatessen sells typical Portuguese products such as confections, wine and olive oil. Located near Bolhão Market.

Arcádia €€

Traditional chocolatier of Porto since 1933, with several locations in Porto (Boavista, Rua do Almada, Rua Santa Catarina). Known for its bonbons and 'cat tongues' and Drageias de Licor Bonjour. Eight locations in the Porto area.

Chocolataria Equador €€

Portuguese chocolatier founded 2009, with strong links to São Tomé and Príncipe. Aims to be independent from negative global practices and involved in the process from bean to bar. Three locations in downtown Porto.

Leitaria da Quinta do Paço €

Originating as a dairy in Paços de Ferreira in 1920, it began making eclairs in the 1950s and grew from there. Six locations in the Porto area, mostly in shopping centres.

🏬 Market Meanders

Mercado do Bolhão

Under renovation since March 2018, the vendors of fish, meat, produce and regional products temporarily installed nearby eagerly await the city's municipal building completion.

Mercado de Matosinhos

Renovated in 2013 and faithful to the original structure, this two-level, four-entrance building houses a fish market, chickens, rabbits, bio products, restaurants, shops and offices.

Praia dos Ingleses

🍴 Food Hall Buzz

Mercado Beira-Rio

No longer a traditional municipal market in Lower Gaia, it resembles more of a food hall with kiosks operated as extensions of restaurants and food shops. Great for sampling various foods.

Mercado do Bom Sucesso

Once a traditional market, the exterior remains the same but vendors are now mostly food- and beverage-related. Hosts book fairs and occasional live-music events.

☀ Beach Day Out

Praia dos Ingleses, Foz

Plenty of amenities around, accessible by public transit (Bus 500 or 202) or on foot. Can be busy due to its convenient location.

Praia de Matosinhos

A 20-minute metro ride away from Porto centre (Metro Matosinhos Sul). Find a beach bar and watch beach volleyball, surfing, and the cruise ships go by at the Porto de Leixões.

Praia de Miramar, Vila Nova de Gaia

Home of the chapel on the beach, Capela do Senhor da Pedra. A half-hour train ride away from São Bento Railway Station.

Praia da Madalena, Vila Nova de Gaia

One of Gaia's most popular beaches on the other side of the Douro. Take Bus 901 or 906 from Casa da Música: the line terminates at the beach.

🔲 Urban Art

Mira by Daniel Eime

Mural in Miragaia using stencils and portraying the aged population from that part of the city.

Steak 'n Shake by Joana Vasconcelos

Mural with 8000 hand-painted tiles commissioned by Steak 'n Shake.

Look at Porto by Vhils

Mural in Miragaia, on the Look at Porto 5D Cinema building. The artist, Vhils, carved the white parts of the wall to produce this mural.

Half-Rabbit by Bordallo II

A magnificent sculpture several stories in height, built from recycled garbage installed at the corner of a building in one of the back streets from Cais de Gaia

Don Quixote by Mesk, Fedor and Mots

One of the first large-scale licensed murals in the city, near Porto's main art street, Rua Miguel Bombarda near Rua de Cedofeita.

Trindade mural by Hazul and Mr Dheo

The first big mural commissioned by the City of Porto from two of its most popular street artists at the time welcomes people as they leave Trindade Metro Station.

Modern Religion by Mr Dheo

To counter the negativity usually associated with social housing, the city commissioned artists to paint murals in some of the buildings in Francos and Carvalhido. This piece is in Francos.

AN.FI.TRI.ÃO by Frederico Draw Alice Luísa Santos and Luísa Vieira de Sousa

Painted on the walls of a building behind the Sé, welcoming to the city anyone crossing the top of Ponte Luís I from Vila Nova de Gaia.

📷 Modern Architecture

Casa da Música

The 'House of Music' is an artistic, cultural and social venue designed by Dutch architect Rem Koolhaas for Porto 2001 European Capital of Culture. Guided visits daily, also in English, French and Spanish.

Cruise Terminal of the Porto de Leixões

Receiving cruise ships since 2011, the terminal was completed in 2015. Also has marina facilities, UPTEC/University of Porto, event rooms and restaurant. Guided tours on Sunday mornings (€5) from 9.30am to noon.

Serralves Villa

Located on the grounds managed by the Serralves Foundation in Boavista, the Villa is an example of 1930s art deco. Former residence of Count Carlos Alberto Cabral. Visits part of General Ticket.

ARCHITECT: REM KOOLHAAS NITPICKER/SHUTTERSTOCK ©

Casa da Música

⁂ Local Events

Festas de Senhor de Matosinhos

Celebrated usually for several weeks in May, there's live music, street food, daily markets and an amusement park. This is an event for the whole family.

Festas de São João

The *santos populares* (popular saints) get their own day and St John's is celebrated on the eve of 23 June. Grill those sardines and get out your squeaky plastic hammer, this is Porto's biggest party of the year. On 24 June there's a regatta on the Douro River, a race between the port wine houses in their *rabelo* boats.

Festas de São Pedro

The end of June, usually, is when tiny São Pedro de Afurada (Vila Nova de Gaia) celebrates St Peter with a parade, concerts and a street party.

Festa do Outono, Serralves

October harvest festival program for the whole family, with free access to the grounds.

ᴪᴪ Family Days

Zoo de Santo Inácio

A zoo built for the animals but also with families in mind, including picnic areas and restaurants. Visit all the different habitats in one entertaining day.

Parque Biológico, Vila Nova de Gaia

Cheaper than a visit to the zoo but just as educational. Find out more about the different animals and plants local to this region.

Festas de São João

Clube de Minigolfe do Porto

Located at Jardim do Passeio Alegre, Foz (€2.5 for 18 holes). Have fun playing golf with your kids while watching the boats pass by.

World of Discoveries

An interactive museum that presents Portugal's contribution to the exploration of the oceans and new routes to new worlds. Located across from the Alfândega.

Parque de Serralves

The Serralves Foundation organises the harvest festival and some workshops for families. Alternatively, go for a treetop walk (p179) or visit the farm animals.

Sea Life Porto

Walk through a tunnel under the main oceanic aquarium; find out more about other aquatic habitats including the Douro River and others around the world.

PORTO REVIEWS

Scan to find more things to do in Porto online

33 Pilgrimage to BRAGA

RECREATION | SPIRITUAL | VIEWS

It's no coincidence that many of Portugal's shrines are placed at the top of mountains, to be closer to the heavens and the divine. For Braga, the city with the oldest cathedral in Portugal, the small nearby mountains are a beacon for devout pilgrims and restful, reflective places for others.

TRABANTOS/SHUTTERSTOCK ©

🗺️ How to

Pedestrian pilgrimage from Braga Railway Station to Bom Jesus do Monte 5.5km to the upper town, then 500 steps to the sanctuary.

Other ways of getting to Bom Jesus do Monte By car it's 60km total from Porto; it's 10 minutes from Braga Railway Station to the top. By city bus it's 20 minutes from Braga Railway Station (€1.55). By funicular it's 274m (2½ to four minutes) between the upper town and the sanctuary (€1.50 one way/€2.50 return).

ALTOSVIC/SHUTTERSTOCK ©

LUISCOSTINHAA/SHUTTERSTOCK ©

Bom Jesus do Monte Overlooking the city of Braga is Bom Jesus do Monte (bomjesus.pt), located on Mt Espinho, a small mountain considered sacred and a key pilgrimage site with roots in the 14th century. The mountain is crowned with a 600-year-old sanctuary and a Baroque-styled religious complex of ornamental gardens, fountains, sculptures and woodland park.

The vantage point is well worth the climb up the grand staircase, subdivided into three stairways with terraces dedicated to the five senses and five virtues. The celebrated **Stairway of the Five Senses** was built from 1725 onwards. With its walls, steps, fountains, statues and other ornamental elements, it is the most symbolic of the Baroque works in the complex. The six fountains have allegorical figures, five fountains representing each of the senses and one fountain combining all of them. The **Stairway of the Virtues**, built in the second half of the 18th century, follows the five senses. The church (constructed from 1784 to 1811) has a neo-classical facade and two bell towers.

If you would rather save your lungs than climb the staircase to the top, take the historic **funicular** (1882), the oldest in the world operated by a water counterbalancing system.

Sanctuary of Our Lady of Sameiro Our Lady of Sameiro is a domed sanctuary from the 19th century, the second largest Marian devotional shrine in Portugal, after the Sanctuary of Fátima. As with Bom Jesus, it's built atop a mountain, at 566m, with grand views overlooking the valley surrounding Braga. In front of the sanctuary is a majestic and vast stairway, at the top of which are the monuments of the Sacred Heart of Jesus and of Our Lady of the Conception.

Left Sanctuary of Our Lady of Sameiro **Far left top** Bom Jesus do Monte **Far left bottom** Funicular

⊘ Unesco World Heritage

In 2019, the sanctuary and religious complex of Bom Jesus do Monte in Braga was added to Unesco's World Heritage List of sites for its recreation of a sacred mount crowned with a church; a kind of Christian Jerusalem. It was in this same year that renovation works of the site were completed, giving a facelift to the centuries-old granite buildings and their whitewashed plaster facades, framed by exposed stonework.

Amazing Arouca
GEOPARK

NATURE | ADVENTURE | HIKING

▬▬▬ Rocky landscapes, river rapids and flora-veiled mountains welcome you to Northern Portugal's Unesco Arouca Geopark. Over forty geological attractions await scientific explorers, ranging from trace fossils to giant trilobites, while a network of fourteen marked trails traverse the landscape.

PAULOMACHADO_9/SHUTTERSTOCK ©

🗺 How to

Getting here & around Driving to Arouca town takes one hour from Porto. Bus connections are approximately two hours with a change in São João da Madeira (€5.40; transdev.pt). To explore the park, utilise hiking routes, tours, taxis or self-drive.

When to go The walkways and bridge close on certain holidays. Spring and autumn are the most pleasant times for hiking. Snow can arrive on the coldest days.

Learn more The friendly Interactive Tourism Office provides maps for trails. (aroucageopark.pt)

DE VISU/SHUTTERSTOCK ©

FILIPE PIMENTEL/SHUTTERSTOCK ©

SIDE TRIP ADVENTURES IN AROUCA GEOPARK

Left Floral carpet, Arouca Geopark **Far left top** Paiva walkway steps **Far left bottom** Ponte 516 Arouca

Paiva walkways The serene soundtrack of river rapids and birdsong accompany you along the Passadiços do Paiva – Arouca's most treasured attraction. A near nine-kilometre linear trail of boardwalks, gravel tracks and wooden staircases follow the Paiva River, starting or ending at either Areinho (enter here if you wish to tackle the steepest stairs first) or Espiunca. River beaches, toilets and snacks can be found at either end, and also halfway at Praia Fluvial do Vau – while waterfalls and Geosites, marked by information boards and QR codes, can be studied along the three-hour route. Taxis between trailheads and Arouca usually wait at both ends (€15 to €23), with the transfer time approximately 20 minutes. (passadicosdopaiva.pt)

Ponte 516 Arouca Laying claim to being the world's longest pedestrian suspension bridge since opening in 2021, this 516-metre marvel of engineering stretches across the Paiva River. Crossing the metal grid-tray system 175m above the river is an exhilarating experience, and for those who dare, the views are reward enough. (516arouca.pt)

River rafting adventures Once you've conquered the heights, and traversed the river walkways, add a little more adrenaline at water level by riding the rapids. Choose from rafting, canoeing and even river trekking by joining the local watersports club for a day. (clubedopaiva.com)

Booking & costs Tickets for Ponte 516 Arouca (€12 including the walkways) and Paiva Walkways (€2) are reserved online in advance.

The Park Beyond Paiva

Arouca town Marvel at the 17th-century Monastery and Sacred Art Museum, savour *Castanhas Doce* sweets or Arouquesa beef, and shop boutique stores for local handicrafts.

Hiking & biking Fourteen scenic trails cover various themes – such as geosites, waterfalls, cliffs or mines.

Panorâmica do Detrelo da Malhada Admire the spectacular verdant views over Serra da Freita from this raised platform.

Pedras Parideiras Interpretation Centre Learn more about the rare and fascinating process of granitisation from a 'mother' stone.

Canyoning & climbing Climb the rugged terrain in the Freita Mountain plateau or tackle one of nine canyoning routes through the park.

DOURO VALLEY

OUTDOORS | VITICULTURE | VIEWS

Experience Douro Valley online

DOURO VALLEY
Trip Builder

Not just for wine lovers, the region offers a range of activities in every season, from summer vineyard events and guided museum visits to rejuvenating spring hikes. Relax in nature or feast on local gastronomy: the Valley's hospitality is legendary.

Glide up the Douro in a traditional **rabelo boat** (p203)
🕐 ½ day

Slumber luxuriously in a **Quinta da Pacheca** wine barrel (p207)
🕐 1 day

Ramble the trails between ancient villages, then stop to break bread in **Favaios** (p209)
🕐 1 day

Vila Real

Alijó

Favaios

TRÁS-OS-MONTES E ALTO DOURO

Provesende

Gouvães do Douro

Pinhão

Rio Douro

Tua

Rio Tua

Galafura

Gouvinhas

Covas do Douro

Peso da Régua

Covelinhas

Rio Douro

Valença do Douro

São João de Pesqueira

Folgosa

Adorigo

Join the Purple Feet Club: stomp grapes at **Santa Eufêmia** (p206)
🕐 ½ day

BEIRA ALTA

Ride the vintage rails of the **Douro Historical Train** (p203)
🕐 ½ day

0 — 10 km
0 — 5 miles

Practicalities

ARRIVING

Francisco Sá Carneiro Airport (OPO) is the closest airport, 100km from the Douro Valley.

Peso da Régua is a port city and hub for arrivals by train, boat, car and coach.

FIND YOUR WAY

Internet can be spotty in the Upper Douro; download a map locally in your GPS system or grab a detailed map in Peso da Régua.

MONEY

ATMs can be few and far between in the countryside. Carry enough cash for meals in small, family-run restaurants.

WHERE TO STAY

Location	Atmosphere
Peso da Régua	Lots of lodgings; conveniently close to transport links
Pinhão	Some options in Pinhão proper; many superb properties a short taxi ride away
Lamego	Wider variety of accommodation, from secluded wine hotels to guesthouses in town
Vila Nova de Foz Côa	Charming rural lodges within half an hour's drive

EATING & DRINKING

Wine The choices are endless in wine country.

Traditional bread in Favaios is a bun with four corners.

Must-try convent sweets made with local almonds such as *tarte de amêndoa*.

Best bola de carne arguably *bola de carne de vinha d'alhos* of Lamego (the meat is marinated in wine and garlic).

GETTING AROUND

Driving is the best way to visit the region.

Trains run on one line starting in Porto, following the Douro River on the north side, ending at Pocinho.

Intercity buses use a hub-and-spoke system, with Viseu the south hub and Vila Real the north hub.

JAN–MAR	**APR–JUN**	**JUL–SEP**	**OCT–DEC**
Winter temps reach freezing overnight, March is moderate	Best season to visit, especially April and May	Scorching days may curb active pursuits; stay hydrated	Chilly to very cold overnight; daytime temps moderate

DOURO VALLEY FIND YOUR FEET

The Douro River from
ALL ANGLES

TRAIN | BOAT | CAR

▬▬▬ The majesty of the Douro Valley has inspired poetry over centuries, with some of the most dramatic panoramas accessible only by boat from the river. Most visitors take the train or road, but there are sections where neither get close to the water. Here are some sightseeing options to consider.

HERACLES KRITIKOS/SHUTTERSTOCK ©

🗺 How to

Train *Linha do Douro* from Porto to Pocinho (€13.55, around 3½ hours; the only direct train leaves at 9am from São Bento Railway Station in Porto). From Porto, sit on the right side as the train follows the river after Peso da Régua.

Car Avoid weekends in the summer if you wish to drive the EN222 between Peso da Régua and Pinhão as it can get congested.

Rabelo boat Take the morning boat from Pinhão during the summer to avoid the worst heat in the afternoon.

JOSE RUI GALVAO/GETTY IMAGES ©

The views of the Douro River are simply otherworldly between Pinhão and Pocinho, the most scenic section, which can only be seen via car, train or boat cruise that starts in Pinhão.

Train Take the *Linha do Douro* from Porto, one of the most beautiful railway lines in Portugal. It was originally 200km when the full line was open (1872 to 1887), comprising 23 tunnels and 35 bridges. It is now 160km from Porto to Pocinho, the track mostly following the Douro River.

Douro Historical Train Time travel in a steam locomotive and five historical carriages between Peso da Régua and Tua. The line operates June to October. (cp.pt)

Boat From Pinhão to Tua, choose from various types of watercraft, motorised or non-motorised. Departures can take place in the morning or afternoon, with trips from one to two hours or more.

For a vintage experience take a rabelo boat, the traditional wooden cargo boat originally used to transport people and wine along the Douro River.

Car Hire a car and stop at the best viewpoints in the area (p214). The only section where the road is next to the river is between Peso da Régua and Pinhão, but if you choose a week-day during the winter, you'll have it all to yourself. The 27km section of Estrada Nacional 222 between Peso da Régua and Pinhao was awarded the world's best road in 2015. Add your favourite road trip song and you'll want to drive this stretch again and again.

Left Pinhão **Far left top** Rabelo boat on the Douro River **Far left bottom** Barca d'Alva

🛶 Landscapes From a Kayak

Seeing the Douro Valley from a kayak is a profound experience. Paddling past the terraced hills in the morning silence is very special. Between Barca d'Alva and Pocinho where there is no road or train, the silence is only broken by the birds singing and the fish jumping.

Jack Atkinson, *Douro Kayak.* dourokayak.com

A Valley of Gold

**WORLD HERITAGE
WINE REGION**

The Douro Valley is one of Portugal's two Unesco World Heritage wine regions. After 2000 years of wine growing, the region was demarcated by the Marquês de Pombal in 1756 and received heritage status in 2001. The area begins 60km east of Porto and extends 100km to the Spanish border.

The Douro River originates in northwest Spain and flows westward through northern Portugal to Porto, where it empties into the Atlantic. The Portuguese word for gold is *ouro*, suggesting that the name Douro comes from the Portuguese or Spanish for golden.

As one of the oldest demarcated wine regions in the world, the Douro Valley is divided into three subregions: **Baixo Corgo**, the westernmost and smallest in area, is anchored by the city of Peso da Régua and home to many wine producers.

Cima Corgo, the central subregion and the largest in area, is anchored by the town of Pinhão and considered more favourable for port wine production. It is home to large-scale producers such as Dow's (Quinta do Bomfim), Croft (Quinta da Roêda) and Real Companhia Velha (Quinta das Carvalhas).

Douro Superior is the mid-sized, easternmost subregion, the driest of the three, anchored by Vila Nova de Foz Côa.

The Heart & Soul of the Valley

Many people are tempted to stay in Porto and make the Douro Valley a day trip, but you would be remiss if you spent half the day on the roads. Visit the vineyards and don't miss the tastings, but if you have the opportunity to stay longer at a wine estate, chances are you'll meet your hosts, the producers.

The people of the Douro Valley, generations of families, have made it their life's work to learn the art and science of viticulture, merging the products of their land into the local recipes through the processing of olive oils, almonds, fruit, fish and game, in addition to winemaking.

Left View over Douro Superior wine region **Middle** Freshly picked grapes **Right** Autumn colours, Douro Valley

Enotourism

Wine tourism is a growing industry and wine producers are constantly innovating, not only with technology but catering to a wider range of consumer demographics and tastes.

Larger *quintas* (estates) offer more things to do and see than the time-honoured tasting rooms and shops stocking their products – there are spas, workshops for cooking and art, and live entertainment. Offerings of outdoor activities include jeep and helicopter tours, canoeing, kayaking, fishing and birdwatching.

While not having all the trappings of the large producers, the small producers are fiercely proud of their work and will reward your visit with personalised attention.

> The Portuguese word for gold is ouro, suggesting that the name Douro comes from the Portuguese or Spanish for golden.

🌿 Seasonal Charms

There are two very colourful seasons in the Douro Valley you'll want to photograph: first, in February and March, when the almond, cherry and apple trees explode into blossom. Then, in September and October, when the steep hillsides of vine terraces transform into red and gold. You'll need a passenger to help you navigate while you try not to gawk at the incredible scenery.

Sustainability & Climate Change

A growing number of producers are transitioning to organic farming and more sustainable agricultural practices. Wine tourism can aid this movement by raising the profile of producers using ecological methods and supporting them through direct purchases.

The wine industry is grappling with the effects of climate change in the form of extreme weather events, prompting Douro Valley producers to hold Climate Change Leadership conferences in Porto to develop solutions for this global issue. Barack Obama and Al Gore were keynote speakers in 2018 and 2019.

36

A Path of Wine
ESTATES

TRADITION | WINE | ESTATES

The wine producers of the Douro Valley number in the thousands, from tiny operations closed to the public to large, established estates opened year-round to visits. How to choose? We have selected five notable wine estates, listing them geographically from west to east.

DOURO VALLEY EXPERIENCES

PEDRO QUARTIN GRACA/SHUTTERSTOCK ©

🗺 Trip Notes

Getting around The first three *quintas* (Pacheca, Vallado and Santa Eufémia) are an easy taxi ride apart, while the last two (Bomfim and das Carvalhas) are across the Pinhão Bridge from each other, which can be crossed on foot.

When to go Visit year-round, but during harvest time the grape-stomping is a one-day event, which should not be combined with other visits.

Top tip Eat plenty and hydrate – port wine is 22% alcohol content!

🍇 The Purple Feet Club

Making wine is hard work! The workers sing to make stomping more enjoyable, following the same rhythm and pace to crush the slippery grapes. We recommend staying next to the vines at Santa Eufémia's visitor lodge in Parada do Bispo, which will make it easier to participate.

Vila Real ●

TRÁS-OS-MONTES
E ALTO DOURO

02 Quinta do Vallado is one of the oldest in the Valley with both a traditional house and a modern schist building with pool, gardens and spa. Impressive winery and coveted location.

05 Quinta do Bomfim's prized wines demonstrate their obsession with the winemaking process. Located in Upper Douro, the estate is both traditional and contemporary, with quality tours and tastings.

○ Provesende

Galafura ○

Gouvinhas ○

Covas do ○
Douro

Pinhão ○

Peso da Régua

Covelinhas ○

Rio Douro

Valença
do Douro

○ Folgosa

○ Adorigo

03 Quinta de Santa Eufémia is a relatively small, seventh-generation producer next to a charming, newly refurbished chapel. Observe their entire production line through glass; if timed right, it's possible to arrange grape-stomping.

04 Quinta das Carvalhas is a classic wine estate with unique views of the Douro River. It's possible to spend the whole day there with activities – they even have a birdwatching program.

BEIRA
ALTA

01 Take a relaxed tour of 18th-century **Quinta da Pacheca** followed by a wine tasting, and stay in one of the *quinta's* 10 giant barrels (pictured left) – more luxurious than you'd think!

N
0   5 km
0   2.5 miles

37
Wine Villages
RECLAIMED

OUTDOORS | VILLAGES | HIKING

In 2001, when the Douro wine region was given Unesco World Heritage status, a project with the aim of recovering several wine villages was born. Six villages were chosen for rehabilitation: two of them on the north side of the Douro, four of them on the south, all with the Douro countryside as their backdrop.

MICHAEL MELFORD/GETTY IMAGES ©

🗺 How to

Getting here It is easier to get around by car; there is no bus service to these small villages.

When to go It can get insanely hot for hiking in the summer. Spring and autumn are the best months for temperature and flora.

For tranquil walks Avoid the peak of the harvest season: vineyards are busy and with all the machinery it can get quite noisy.

VR2000/SHUTTERSTOCK ©

Far left top Favaios Far left bottom Ucanha bridge

Provesende This rural wine village was once the seat of a municipality. It boasts several manor houses, most notably Morgadio da Calçada, which is partly open to the public. Other points of interest include the pillory, the 17th-century fountain, the 18th-century church of St Marinha, and the Portuguese-Roman cemetery at Quinta da Relva.

Trevões Traditional shoe-making is still alive and well here. The historic centre has ancient houses and two museums, one dedicated to the village and countryside, the other to religious art.

Barcos Sloping above the Távora River, Barcos is known for its views and the 12th-century church with interesting porticos, one of the best examples of late-Romanic architecture.

For an easy amble, the villages of Salzedas and Ucanha are less than 3km apart with a maximum of 100m elevation change:

Salzedas has an impressive monastery of the Cistercian Order whose construction first began in 1168 and expanded in the 17th and 18th centuries. Try the Salzedas Biscuit (Biscoito de Salzedas), the traditional recipe of the Cistercian monks who also made elderberry liqueur.

Ucanha One of the oldest settlements in the region, the village is unique in Portugal for its toll tower and medieval fortified bridge over the Varosa River. Stop by the church of São João Evangelista and the ruins of the Old Abbey.

🍷 Bread & Wine of Favaios

The village of **Favaios** may be small, but it's become a favourite stop for visitors to the Douro Valley.

Visit the **Favaios Wine Cooperative** (Adega Cooperativa de Favaios) to sample Moscatel wine and learn about its production.

The informative **Bread and Wine Museum** (Núcleo Museológico Favaios, Pão e Vinho) is another place to dive into the history and traditions of the local area. You'll also learn more about moscatel and the process of baking the local specialty, the four-cornered bread. The museum gives tastings of the bread and moscatel produced by the local cooperative.

38 Rocking Your IMAGINATION

ARCHAEOLOGY | NATURE | IMAGINATION

▬▬▬ Côa Valley Archaeological Park, in the Upper Douro where the Côa River branches south, is a 200-sq-km open-air gallery of prehistoric rock art, the largest concentration in the world today. The park was created in 1996 to preserve and manage its exhibition to the public. The expansive Côa Museum was added in 2010.

ARCHITECTS, CAMILO REBELO AND TIAGO PIMENTEL. TAKASHI IMAGES/SHUTTERSTOCK ©

📍 How to

Getting here The closest coach stop is Vila Nova de Foz Côa, about 3km from the museum. The *Linha do Douro* stops at Pocinho train station, 7km from Vila Nova de Foz Côa. The *Linha da Beira Alta* stops at Celorico da Beira train station, 60km from Vila Nova de Foz Côa.

Prearrange visits Visiting the archaeological sites is only possible by prearrangement with the museum.

ANDERS BLOMQVIST/GETTY IMAGES ©

ROBERT SZYMANSKI/SHUTTERSTOCK ©

Left Rock art inscriptions **Far left top** Côa Museum **Far left bottom** Small tour group visiting Canada do Inferno rock engravings

DOURO VALLEY EXPERIENCES

The large and modern **Côa Museum** is situated on a rocky outcrop at the intersection of two Unesco World Heritage sites where the rivers Côa and Douro meet. Digital media exhibitions illustrate the art of the prehistoric engravers to complement the major works, the archaeological sites. The museum also has a restaurant.

There are three main sites to visit: **Canada do Inferno, Penascosa** and **Ribeira de Piscos**. In addition to the rock art sites open to the public, there are other archaeological sites nearby worth visiting: roman and medieval ruins, castles and remnants of other settlements.

Kayak visits to Canada do Inferno or Fariseu combine a relaxing leisure activity with rock art, flora and fauna. Fariseu boasts the largest outdoor engraving of 3.5m, which can only be viewed by kayak.

Canada do Inferno and Ribeira de Piscos are visited only during the morning, when the panels are illuminated by the sun. For the same reason, the engraved panels at Penascosa are visited only in the afternoon. Night visits, which use light and shadow to make the engravings stand out, are only available at Penascosa. Note that visits to Penascosa depart from the village of Castelo Melhor, at the park's reception centre.

Bouncing in a 4WD at the edge of steep ravines feels like going on a safari, with eagles and vultures circling overhead. The protected park is home to various species of flora and fauna, mostly undisturbed by human contact. There's an aura of mystique owing to its wild, rugged nature.

🚶 Right This Way

The only access to the archaeological sites at Parque Côa is by prior arrangement with the museum, who limit the number of visitors for conservation and practical reasons. Visits to the three main sites can be undertaken on foot along marked pedestrian trails, through organised kayak trips, or excursions in all-terrain vehicles followed by a walk to the engravings.

The museum guides have specialised training and can identify and explain the etchings in the schist rock. These are mainly of the early animals that roamed the Côa Valley, namely aurochsen (a species of wild cattle), horses, goats and deer species.

FLAVOURS
of the Douro

01 Biscoito da Teixeira

From the parish of Teixeira, they're a dark rectangular shape, flavoured with lemon and traditionally baked in a wood-burning oven.

02 Presunto de Lamego

Lamego is known for its smoked meats (*presunto* is ham).

03 Ensopado de Borrego

Stew made with native Terrincho lamb.

04 Rebuçados da Régua

Hard candies sold out of baskets at the Peso da Régua train station.

05 Marrã de Mesão Frio

Pork meat cooked with red wine.

06 Ensopado de Javali (Upper Douro)

Stewed wild boar, poured over old bread.

07 Cristas de galo (Vila Real)

Rooster crest with egg custard from Santa Clara Convent.

08 Pitos de Santa Luzia (Vila Real)

A pastry filled with pumpkin jam.

09 Carne de vinha d'alhos de Mesão Frio

Meat marinated in a wine, garlic and vinegar sauce.

10 Migas de Peixe do Rio

A bread broth from Foz do Sabor with river fish.

11 Tigelinhas de laranja (Vila Real)

'Little orange bowls' made with citrus and almond.

12 Other convent sweets (Vila Real)

Bexigas (bladders), the *santórios* (sanctuaries; pictured right), and the *ganchas de S. Brás* (Claws of S. Brás; pictured left) made from sugar and water.

Listings

BEST OF THE REST

🏰 Castles in the Douro

Lamego

Medieval castle documented since the 10th century. This is the highest point in Lamego with the best views of the Coura, Balsemão and Varosa Rivers. Today what remains is the keep (tower) and walls.

Freixo de Espada à Cinta

One of the oldest castles in the area, documented since the 13th century. Today there are some remains of the old fortress, mainly the seven-sided Torre do Galo.

Numão

Medieval castle dating back to the days of Christian Reconquest and impressively illuminated at night. It's believed that the castle once had 15 towers and was often visited by kings.

☀ Events & Festivals

Festa da Amendoeira em Flor de Vila Nova Foz Côa

The Almond Blossom Route *(Rota das Amendoeiras em Flor)* puts on a show in late February to early March when the Douro Valley snows blossoms. It is a wonder to behold, driving from Vila Nova de Foz Côa, Capital of Almond Trees, to Barca d'Alva. This coincides with the annual two-week festival program hosted by Vila Nova Foz Côa, culminating in a parade on the last day.

Vindouro – the Pombaline Festival (São João da Pesqueira)

Three days in late August to early September celebrating wine: competitions, auctions, tastings and an 18th-century street market.

Other activities include concerts, a traditional Pombaline market, parade, and dinner prepared by a well-known Portuguese chef. On the last day, 1 September, there's an auction of historic wines.

Romaria da Nossa Senhora dos Remédios (Lamego)

A large-scale event from late August to early September in Lamego, in honour of Our Lady of Remedies. There are fireworks, shows and the Procession of the Triumph by pilgrims on 8 September.

👀 Miradouros Over the Douro

São Leonardo da Galafura

Thirty minutes by car from Peso da Régua and 640m high, the view was an inspiration for the Portuguese poet Miguel Torga (real name Adolfo Correia da Rocha).

Casal de Loivos

Between Pinhão and Alijó in the village of the same name, where the vineyards, farms and villages hug the river and form a landscape that will take your breath away.

HOMYDESIGN/SHUTTERSTOCK ©

Numão

Fraga do Puio

Located in Picote, the viewpoint is within the Parque Natural do Douro Internacional along the border between Portugal and Spain. The balcony was rebuilt in 2017 in glass and wood.

São Salvador do Mundo

Located at a height of 493m near São João da Pesqueira, the vista overlooks the Douro Valley and its smaller rivers, the dam and the Cachão Valeira.

Rota do Douro

Located between Beira and Coleja, across from Quinta das Vargellas and Vargellas railway station, with magnificent views over the villages and vineyards.

 **Dining With Flair**

DOC, Folgosa €€€

The crème de la crème of dining experiences in the Douro is by Chef Rui Paula, who's received Michelin stars twice since 2017. DOC (Degustar Ousar Comunicar; Taste Dare Communicate) opened in 2007 and has a coveted view of the river. The menu is a reflection of the valley's abundance and seasonality.

Cozinha da Clara, Pinhão €€€

Executive Chef Pedro Cardoso started Cozinha da Clara in 2017. Part of the wine estate Quinta de la Rosa near Pinhão, it prides itself on using produce from its own garden and sourcing ingredients as locally as possible, and has a menu which leans contemporary.

Wine House Restaurant, Lamego €€€

Chef Carlos Pires heads the restaurant located in Quinta da Pacheca, in a rural setting opposite Peso da Régua on the left bank. The restaurant menu is Mediterranean and traditional Portuguese, with world influences such as French and Japanese styles weaving their way in.

Museu de Lamego

TRABANTOS/SHUTTERSTOCK ©

DOURO VALLEY REVIEWS

🏛 **Museum Picks**

Museu do Douro, Peso da Régua

Completed in 2008, this regional museum in a renovated 18th-century building represents the wine region's collective identity and cultural attributes. It houses a permanent collection and an exhibition space, plus a restaurant, a store, an information centre, a reading room, a wine bar and an esplanade in a garden with a view of the Douro River.

Côa Museum, Vila Nova de Foz Côa

Opened in 2010, the museum has four floors of permanent and temporary exhibitions dedicated to the prehistoric rock art of the Côa Valley, and the environment of hunter-gatherer societies in the Paleolithic era.

Museu de Lamego

Once an episcopal palace, the museum is in the historic centre of Lamego and was inaugurated in 1917. It contains an eclectic collection of artifacts from photography to transport, textiles to paintings.

 Scan to find more things to do in the Douro Valley online

TRÁS-OS-MONTES

OUTDOORS | HISTORY | LOCAL HERITAGE

Experience Trás-os-Montes online

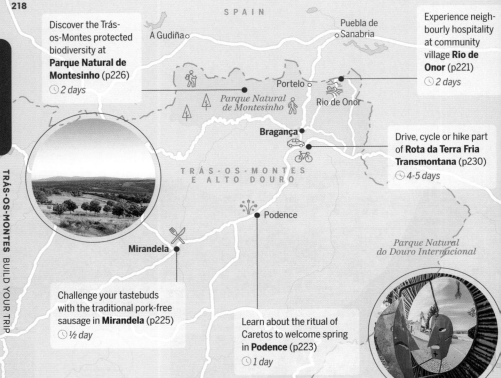

SPAIN

Discover the Trás-os-Montes protected biodiversity at **Parque Natural de Montesinho** (p226)
🕐 2 days

A Gudiña

Puebla de Sanabria

Experience neighbourly hospitality at community village **Rio de Onor** (p221)
🕐 2 days

Portelo

Parque Natural de Montesinho

Rio de Onor

Bragança

Drive, cycle or hike part of **Rota da Terra Fria Transmontana** (p230)
🕐 4-5 days

TRÁS-OS-MONTES E ALTO DOURO

Podence

Parque Natural do Douro Internacional

Mirandela

Challenge your tastebuds with the traditional pork-free sausage in **Mirandela** (p225)
🕐 ½ day

Learn about the ritual of Caretos to welcome spring in **Podence** (p223)
🕐 1 day

TRÁS-OS-MONTES
Trip Builder

▬▬ The Northeast's isolated location and infamous weather have created an intriguing cultural identity. Embrace the *transmontano* lifestyle, exploring protected natural parks or ancient pagan celebrations.

MATT MUNRO/LONELY PLANET ©
LUISCOSTINHAA/SHUTTERSTOCK ©

0   20 M
0   10 miles
Ⓝ

Practicalities

ARRIVING

Francisco Sá Carneiro Airport (OPO) is the closest, a three-hour drive via the A4 motorway.

Express buses from Porto and Lisbon serve most of the main towns.

CONNECT

Good wi-fi coverage. Double-check your plan fees: near the border, your phone might pick up a Spanish carrier's signal.

MONEY

Carry cash for small purchases at local shops. Chain stores and other businesses accept most debit and credit cards.

WHERE TO STAY

Location	Atmosphere
Bragança	The district's capital city; mix of boutique hotels and well-known international chains
Rio de Onor	Picturesque, self-catered rural homes for short-term rent; community lifestyle in the village
Vinhais	Camping at Parque Biológico de Vinhais; free facilities; bring your campervan or your tent, or stay at bungalows

EATING & DRINKING

Feijoada à transmontana A hearty bean-based stew cooked with cabbage and smoked meats.

Castanha da Terra Fria Locally produced chestnuts, DOP (Designated Protected Origin).

Winemaking, Valpaços sub-region Fruity and floral whites, and robust and balanced reds.

Must-try local dish
Alheira at
O Grês (p232)

Best for Posta
Mirandesa
Gabriela (p232)

GETTING AROUND

Driving is the best way to get to know Trás-os-Montes, via a mix of high-speed roads and scenic, undulating secondary toll-free roads cutting through the mountainous landscape.

Long-distance buses depart with some regularity from Lisbon and Porto to the main cities in the Northeast. A network of almost 80 municipal bus routes connects all cities, towns and villages in Trás-os-Montes.

TRÁS-OS-MONTES FIND YOUR FEET

JAN–MAR	**APR–JUN**	**JUL–SEP**	**OCT–DEC**
Expect snow in alpine areas and rituals welcoming spring	Mild temps with chilly mornings and evenings, ideal for outdoors	Scorching days call for swims at river beaches	Winter starts to settle in; great for spending time indoors

39 Community VILLAGES

NATURE | COMMUNITY | TRADITION

▬▬ Out of almost two dozen traditional villages scattered all over the Nordeste Transmontano, community life at these four is more prominent and local traditions ignore the passage of time. Isolation brought on by long, hard winters and geographical constraints may have crystallised the way of living of these villagers but haven't detached them from the outside world.

RUI T GUEDES/GETTY IMAGES ©

🗺 How to

Getting here If you're driving, take the A1 (from Lisbon) or the A4 (from Porto). Express buses go as far as the neighbouring cities of Macedo de Cavaleiros and Bragança.

When to go Snowscapes and traditional Carnaval celebrations in February/March make winter the best season to visit.

Experience village life Briefly become part of the community by staying at a self-catered, independent house (*alojamento local*) in any of the villages.

DIEGO MATTEO MUZZINI/SHUTTERSTOCK ©

Far left top Rio de Onor **Far left bottom** Montesinho

Rio de Onor With less than 100 permanent residents, this tiny village of typical houses and shared oven, farmland and herds is two towns in one. Split by the border, its Spanish side is called Rihonor de Castilla, but locals dismiss political boundaries and divide it into top part (Rihonor) and bottom part (Rio de Onor).

Chacim Located at the foot of Serra de Bornes, it was chosen by royal decree, in the 18th century, to breed silkworms and produce and weave silk. Chacim became one of the main players in Portugal's industrialisation efforts. These days, however, only ruins and memories remain of the old silk factory, Real Filatório de Chacim.

Podence At the end of 2019, this village near Macedo de Cavaleiros jumped to international attention as their traditional way of celebrating Carnaval became officially part of Unesco's Intangible Culture list. The *Entrudo Chocalheiro* is a pagan celebration where men wearing colourful hooded suits and tin or leather masks *(caretos)* bid the long winter farewell and welcome the rejuvenating spring.

Montesinho At about 1030m above sea level, this village in the heart of Parque Natural de Montesinho is one of the highest in Portugal. The houses, some restored and transformed into tourist lodgings, maintain the typical thick granite walls, slate roofs and wooden balconies, ideal to endure the heavy snowfalls in winter.

Explore Beyond the Villages

Visit 'France' without leaving Portugal About 10km separates the villages of Montesinho and France. Weather permitting, hike the marked trail between them among the protected landscapes of the natural park.

Locals' recommended river beach The Praia Fluvial da Ribeira (Azibo river beach) near Podence is a locals' top recommendation. This Blue Flag beach is also equipped for beachgoers with reduced mobility.

Build your own Careto mask The recovered farm-turned-hotel Quinta do Pomar (quintado pomar.com) houses a workshop where visitors can see how a Careto mask is made and give a shot at it themselves.

Mirandese & Caretos

MAURICIO ABREU/ALAMY STOCK PHOTO ©

AN ANCIENT RITUAL AND PORTUGAL'S SECOND LANGUAGE

In a region as vast as Trás-os-Montes, pinpointing what makes it culturally unique isn't an easy task. But a lot of the region's particular identity comes through in these two separate cultural aspects: Mirandese, Portugal's other official language, and Carnival of Podence, part of Unesco's Intangible Cultural Heritage since 2019.

Left Herd of goats, Mogadouro
Middle Caretos mask and costume
Right Murals in the streets of Podence

Concerned with preserving their local heritage and unabashedly sticking to their guns when it comes to their ancestry – this neatly sums up the charisma of the *transmontanos*. Surviving in harsh weather, where long and often snowy winters accentuate their geographical isolation from one another and the rest of the country, eventually brought out unparalleled resilience and ingenuity. Turning a once-called-local dialect into Portugal's other official language and putting a unique winter celebration on the cultural map are just a couple of examples of how that flexibility to roll with the punches comes through.

Mirandese: Portugal's Other Official Language

A token of the region's culture and heritage, the 1999 decision to officially recognise Mirandese as a national language was crucial to protect and revitalise the local identity. It also represented a countrywide shakeup as the Portuguese embraced their cultural diversity.

Alcides Meirinhos, writer, Mirandese translator and director of local NGO Associaçon de la Lhéngua i Cultura Mirandesa (ALCM), remembers being teased as a child for 'speaking the local dialect'. City-based folks believed it to be the language of 'the uneducated villagers who didn't know how to speak proper Portuguese'.

Today, hearing locals speaking Mirandese on a daily basis might be difficult to witness because most speakers only communicate in the local language among themselves, and often only outside the main towns and cities. But stroll through the counties of Miranda do Douro, Mogadouro or Vimioso and you'll come across street plaques and road signs in both Portugal's official languages.

Although it's no longer considered the language of the unschooled and ageing rural communities, Mirandese has yet to reach global status as it's not fluently spoken by the younger generations. Statistical data accounts for up to 15,000 native speakers, 3000 of them in Portugal. Learning the language is optional in local schools, hindering the preservation of Mirandese.

> *Unabashedly sticking to their guns when it comes to their ancestry – this neatly sums up the charisma of the transmontanos.*

From Podence to the World

The Carnaval de Podence jumped from local celebration to global cultural event when in 2019 it was inscribed in Unesco's list of Intangible Cultural Heritage of Humanity. It's hard to pinpoint how old these winter festivities are, but it's certain they are a Roman or Celtic rite of passage and a pagan celebration to welcome spring and the end of a long winter.

'Emigration, the Colonial War and the dictatorial political regime in the 1970s almost made the tradition disappear completely. The documentary film *Máscaras* (Noémia Delgado, 1976) helped bring it back to life.' António Carneiro, the president and founding member of local cultural organisation Caretos de Podence, says that today 'younger generations are immensely proud of their roots and traditions, carrying on the legacy'.

For four days – ending on Shrove Tuesday – men dress up in colourful costumes, hide their identity behind *caretos* (leering masks) and recreate the ancient rite of passage: dancing around the women while shaking the cowbells tied around their waists.

Cultural Evolution & Preservation

Learn the language Paid online courses are available through ALCM's website. Knowing Portuguese or being based in Portugal is not a pre-requisite. (lhengua.org)

Mirandese in pop culture Several books have been translated into Mirandese, including Asterix and Obelix comics and Saint-Exupéry's *The Little Prince*. Wikipedia's Mirandese version (Biquipédia) was launched in 2009.

Inclusive tradition in Podence Although traditionally the Caretos and their rituals were a rite of passage for men, the celebrations are now open to include women and children.

Caretos board game MEBO, a board-game company based in Portugal, have launched a Caretos-inspired board game.

40 Cuisine & Craft
TRADITIONS

FOOD | ARTS | CULTURE

More than just learning what local dishes to try or selecting must-buy traditional crafts, embrace this experience as a close encounter with the local culture. Flavours and craftsmanship bring out Nordeste Transmontano's people's resilience and their resolve in keeping their traditions alive.

HORACIO VILLALOBOS/GETTY IMAGES ©

🗺 How to

Getting here Driving is your best bet, as all villages, towns and cities are connected by an intricate network of motorways and secondary roads.

When to go Local celebrations, which involve food and traditional cultural events, are at their peak during winter.

Alternative foods Traditional cuisine is meat- and game-heavy, but it's possible to find vegetarian alternatives to some staple dishes.

BRUNO ISMAEL SILVA ALVES/SHUTTERSTOCK ©

Left Artisanal knives, Palaçoulo **Far left top** Members of Pauliteiros de Miranda **Far left bottom** *Alheiras*

Well-Seasoned Local Culture

A deceiving sausage When, in the 15th century, Iberian Jews were forced to convert to Christianity or face persecution, most became New Christians on paper but continued to practice their religion in secret. The absence of a staple dish like pork in someone's household would raise suspicion. So, the Jewish community in Mirandela invented *alheira*. Another version, though, states the sausage was born out of scarcity of the usual main ingredient. Poultry and bread replace pork in this garlicky, paprika-flavoured traditional dish.

Unattractive but delicious Made with bean pods and a strange-looking sausage, *butelo com cascas* is a traditional stew in which the smoked flavours make up for the lack of love at first sight.

From a village to the world Of the almost 600 people who live in Palaçoulo, a town in Miranda do Douro near the Spanish border, most live off the cutlery and barrel-making industries. Instead of giving in to their geographical isolation, villagers made the best of their traditional knowledge, turning artisanal knives and wine barrels into a booming, internationally famous business.

Northeastern music instruments Traditionally built and played by shepherds, the Mirandese bagpipes are one of the rarest and oldest of their kind in Europe. They're part of many traditional cultural events' soundtrack and have made their way into the contemporary Portuguese music scene.

🍴 Local Feasts & Festivals

Feira do Fumeiro Vinhais, self-proclaimed capital of smoked meats, hosts, every February, an event solely dedicated to local sausages. (fumeirodevinhais.pt)

Festival do Butelo e das Casulas The peculiar bean pods and sausage stew is the main attraction of this gastronomic event in Bragança, but festival-goers will also be able to indulge in other local delicacies.

Pauliteiros de Miranda True to their Celtic roots, Pauliteiros replaced swords with sticks in a traditional dance to the sound of local bagpipes. In addition to an ongoing application for Unesco's Intangible Cultural Heritage list, the ensemble represented Northern Portugal at Expo 2020 Dubai.

41 Outdoor
DELIGHTS

STARS | SNOWSCAPES | BIODIVERSITY

Prepare to ditch the stress of urban life at the country's largest protected area, Parque Natural de Montesinho. Meander through the picture-worthy landscapes of the Portuguese Northeast, hike or cycle the marked paths, observe the resident wildlife, gaze at starry skies or enjoy the first snowfalls.

Getting here
Bragança is the city closest to Parque Natural de Montesinho, a 30-minute drive away. Driving is the best way to get around.

When to go Spring and autumn are the sweet-spot seasons for outdoor activities enthusiasts and wildlife connoisseurs. Snowy winters are best for time indoors.

Protected by Unesco
Since 2015 the park has been part of the Meseta Ibérica Transboundary Biosphere Reserve, the largest in Europe.

Animal-spotting

As one of the most biodiverse natural parks in Portugal, Montesinho is the home of almost 70% of the country's total species, some of them endangered. During your wildlife en-counters, planned or otherwise, respect their habitat, give them space, make sure your clothes blend in with the colours around you as much as possible, and admire them from a safe distance.

September to October is mating season for the deer. It's a haunting, one-of-a-kind experience as the sounds of their mating calls echo through the park. To increase your odds of witnessing this event, visit the park early in the morning.

Iberian wolves, one of the aforementioned threatened species, roam freely through the hills of Montesinho, hunting deer and wild

🛏 Overnight in Aldeia de Montesinho

For a fully immersive experience, stay at one of Montesinho village's typical houses, which have been converted into self-catered short-term rentals. In winter, the snow-covered village is even more appealing. During Christmas, witness the ancient pagan rituals cele-brating the winter solstice.

Left Parque Natural de Montesinho **Above left** Montesinho village **Above right** Flock of sheep, Parque Natural de Montesinho

boar, bred to maintain this delicate eco-system. They are one of the most important populations of Iberian wolves in the country.

With more than one hundred resident species of nesting birds, Parque Natural de Montesinho is the chosen permanent address for a few couples of golden eagles. Other birds of prey such as black storks and hen harriers join them in their choice of home.

When treading the hills or the trails, pay close attention to every body of water that you come across. The park houses half of all the reptile and amphibian species living in Portugal.

The resident mammals, such as wildcats, otters, bats and European water voles, take over abandoned mines and mills scattered around the park.

🏛 Explore Beyond the Park

Ancient Roman path
In Moimenta, past the medieval Ponte das Vinhas, notice the relatively well-preserved ancient path, which presumably was first built by the ancient Romans.

Núcleo Interpretativo da Lorga de Dine In Dine, a village about 10km from Parque Natural de Montesinho, visit this local museum showcasing archeological artefacts from the Neolithic period found in the neighbouring cave.

Mel do Parque de Montesinho Honey exclusively produced in Montesinho has boasted the DOP (Protected Designation of Origin) label since 1994 and has been certified organic since 2005. (meldoparque. webnode.pt)

SPAIN

PR7 VNH – Calçada

PR3 BGC – Porto Furado

Escagalhos

Alto do Falgueirão

Moimenta

Rio Sabor

Montesinho

Serra de Montesinho

Parque Natural de Montesinho

Parâmio

Lastra

Rio Baceiro

0 — 5 km
0 — 2.5 miles

Left Roman bridge, Moimenta **Below** Hikers, Parque Natural de Montesinho

Hiking Trails

Parque Natural de Montesinho has two official hiking trails, both circular and ideal for hikers who are okay with a route that is a little challenging. Because the park is a preserved area, travellers must stay on the marked trail at all times.

The **PR3 BGC – Porto Furado** trail begins and ends at the typical village of Montesinho, stretching for 7.8km through valleys, rivers, reservoirs and hilly landscapes. It's the ideal route for nature enthusiasts, more immersive and with fewer stops. The highest peak, Alto do Falgueirão, rises almost 2000m above sea level. At the final stop, before returning to Aldeia de Montesinho, spot the ruins of the Iron Age settlement Castro Curisco.

Starting in Moimenta, the **PR7 VNH – Calçada** trail is the same length as the Porto Furado, but has two more stops, most at human-made landmarks. The mix of attractions on this route favours diverse travelling groups. It balances natural beauties, like the view from Miradouro de Moimenta and the largest forest of oak trees in Europe, with architectural heritage must-sees, like Ponte das Vinhas (a medieval bridge over River Tuela) and Igreja Matriz de Moimenta (the 14th-century main church in the town where the trail ends).

42 Rota da Terra Fria
ENCOUNTER

ROAD TRIP | HIKING | CYCLING

Rota da Terra Fria Transmontana is 455km long, split into 11 pre-designed independent itineraries of varying lengths. But ditch the official map and get a first impression of the Portuguese Northeast while hiking, cycling or driving this condensed, inland itinerary.

ELZAUER/GETTY IMAGES ©

🗺 Trip Notes

Getting here You can start the itinerary in Bragança, a gateway city to the Rota. Get there by bus or car from Lisbon or Porto.

When to go Hikers and cyclists should plan for a spring trip. Summers are scorching, so it's best to travel by car then.

Take the detours The official route map marks detours to unmissable points of interest, from quasi-secret viewpoints to monuments and landmarks.

🥾 Route Within the Route

If you're keen on exploring a less crowded route of Camino de Santiago, it overlaps with Rota da Terra Fria in Sobreiró de Baixo (a 45-minute drive from Bragança). The Portuguese section of Via de la Plata begins there.

04 Take a foodie detour in **Vinhais**, a town known for its smoked meats and hearty soups. In October, locally produced chestnuts are the main stars of food event Rural Castanea.

SPAIN

Parque Natural de Montesinho

Portelo

Vilar Seco de Lomba

Vinhais

Bragança

01 Before heading off, or at the end, carve out time to pay a visit to the 900-year-old medieval castle, protected by a heart-shaped wall (pictured left), in **Bragança**, and the city's historic centre.

05 Near the end of Rota da Terra Fria, in **Vilar Seco de Lomba**, vineyards take over the landscape. Peel your eyes for *bodegas* – wine cellars semi-buried in schist rocks.

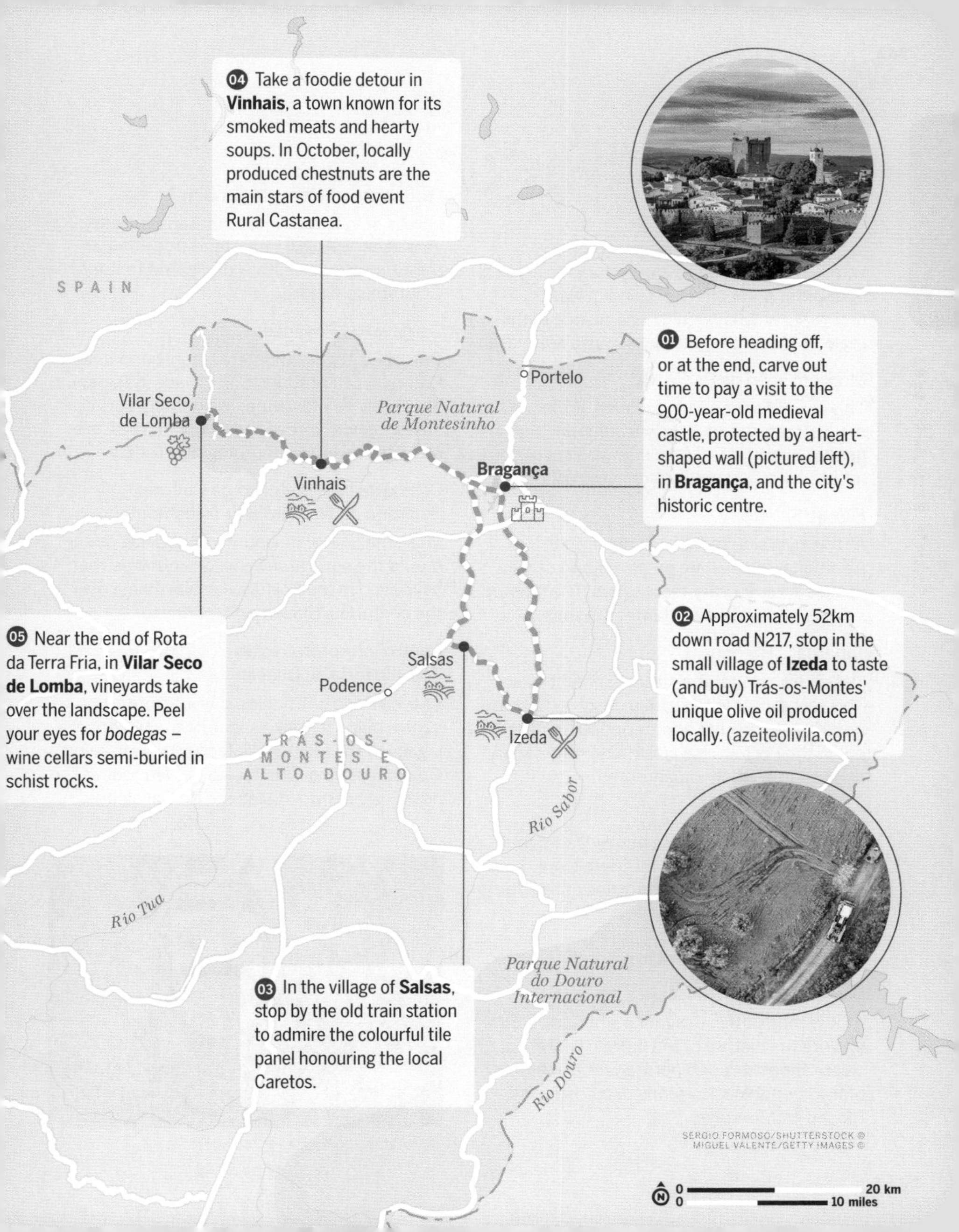

Salsas

Podence

TRÁS-OS-MONTES E ALTO DOURO

Izeda

Rio Sabor

02 Approximately 52km down road N217, stop in the small village of **Izeda** to taste (and buy) Trás-os-Montes' unique olive oil produced locally. (azeiteolivila.com)

Rio Tua

Parque Natural do Douro Internacional

03 In the village of **Salsas**, stop by the old train station to admire the colourful tile panel honouring the local Caretos.

Rio Douro

N   0   20 km
     0   10 miles

Listings

BEST OF THE REST

✕ Local Cuisine

Gabriela €€
Family-owned for almost a century, this typical restaurant at the heart of Sendim was the first to serve what would become one of the region's most famous steaks: *posta Mirandesa*.

Moagem João do Padre €€
This restaurant on Rua do Porto, Podence's main street, serves hearty traditional food in generous portions. Make sure you save room for its well-loved dessert: chestnut pudding.

Flor de Sal €€
At this riverside restaurant in Mirandela, traditional recipes are prepared and served using contemporary techniques. The roasted lamb is one of its most famous dishes.

Taberna O Batoque €
Not all Transmontana cuisine is meat-based. This restaurant in Bragança designed a traditional menu around another popular ingredient in the Portuguese Northeast: vegetarian and vegan-friendly mushrooms.

O Grês €€
Skip asking for the menu at this traditional restaurant in Mirandela, for there's only one dish that makes patrons flock here: the homemade-like *alheira*.

☆ Cultural Immersion

Museu Ibérico da Máscara e do Traje
At this museum in Bragança's historic centre explore the history of the Iberian winter celebrations through permanent exhibitions of traditional masks, props and costumes. Closed on Mondays.

Festival Intercéltico de Sendim
Lovers of folk music head to Sendim every year in early August to attend this 20-year-old international festival dedicated to the Celtic-based genre.

Carnaval de Podence
One of Portugal's most traditional and unique Carnaval celebrations takes place in Podence. The three-day festivities welcoming spring culminate on Shrove Tuesday with the Caretos' parade and the burning of an effigy.

Centro de Interpretação da Cultura Sefardita do Norderdeste Transmontano
This small, local museum in Bragança documents the several Jewish communities that have lived in the Portuguese Northeast over the centuries. Closed on Mondays.

Centro Interpretativo do Real Filatório de Chacim
At the village of Chacim, this interpretative centre helps to make sense of the historical legacy of the former silk factory now in ruins. Open all year round. Book a guided tour at the *posto de turismo* in Macedo de Cavaleitos.

Museu Ibérico da Máscara e do Traje

Walk the wine or Roman routes

Valpaços' city council designed two self-guided walking routes around the region's most important cultural legacies: wineries carved in rocks and ancient Roman roads. (valpacos.pt/pages/555)

⚒ Local Crafts & Food

Cutelaria Martins

Established in 1954, this family-owned factory in Palaçoulo is well known for its customisable artisanal pocket knives. Other types of knives are also available to purchase online or directly at the local store.

Quinta do Pomar

At Podence's main street, in addition to selling local food products, this local *mercearia* sells merchandise related to Caretos: handmade tin and leather masks, cow bells, and the tradition-based board game.

MARRON – Oficina da Castanha

Taste and buy chestnut products at this local business in central Bragança with a museum, a grocery store, and a 30-seat cafeteria where this fruit rules the menu.

Gaita de Foles Mirandesa

The Mirandese bagpipes are part of most of the region's popular music soundtracks. Crafted by hand, the process to build one of these instruments is methodically slow. Célio Pires (Constantim, Miranda do Douro) is one of the most reputable artisans.

⛩ Pre-Historic Settlements

Castro de Sacóias

A 15-minute drive from Bragança, the remains of an Iron Age settlement near Capela Nossa Senhora da Assunção almost go unnoticed. After several restructures, it was presumably occupied last by Roman settlers.

Trás-os-Montes musicians with traditional bagpipes and drums

Miradouro e Povoado Fortificado da Ciradelha

Not much is left of this pre-historic settlement, a 10-minute drive from Vinhais. But the view and the historical information on-site make up for the absence of identifiable remains.

Castro de Ciragata

Also known as Cidadelhe de Parada. The ruins of a defensive wall are visible atop a hill, a short drive from the village of Parada (Bragança district). Archeological findings confirmed its Iron Age origin.

Mamoa de Donai

Practically destroyed megalithic monument 300m to the west of Donai, a village about 10km from Bragança. Resort to locals to pinpoint the exact location of this unmapped landmark.

Abrigos Rupestres do Regato das Bouças

Rock shelters near the Bouças stream in Mirandela, probably used between the Neolithic and Chalcolithic periods, according to the drawings found on-site.

Scan to find more things to do in Trás-os-Montes online

TRÁS-OS-MONTES REVIEWS

Practicalities

ARRIVING

236

GETTING AROUND

238

SAFE TRAVEL

240

MONEY

241

RESPONSIBLE TRAVEL

242

ACCOMMODATION

244

ESSENTIALS

246

LANGUAGE

248

Right Tuk-tuks, Lisbon

EASY STEPS FROM THE AIRPORT TO THE CITY CENTRE

Lisbon is the primary point of entry for most travellers visiting Portugal. The airport is about 6km from the city centre. All flights, domestic and international, arrive at Terminal 1. Terminal 2 is used for departing flights by low-cost carriers. There are some cafes and shops in the arrivals hall, but there is greater variety in the central plaza, on your way to baggage claim.

AT THE AIRPORT

BENNY MARTY/SHUTTERSTOCK ©

SIM CARDS
Cards for unlocked phones can be purchased at the Vodafone Portugal shop at baggage claim (7am to 6pm). However, if you want to compare prices, wait until you've reached the city centre and look for an MEO or NOS shop, the other two Portuguese mobile operators.

CURRENCY EXCHANGE
Unicâmbio offices are located at baggage claim (5am to midnight) and in the arrivals hall (5am to 1am). Exchange fees are two times higher at the airport. If you don't need cash right away, get better prices at other Unicâmbio stores or banks in the city centre.

WI-FI Free wi-fi is available at both terminals, but is usually slow and unreliable. Select _VINCI Airports WiFi and follow the prompts.

ATMS Teller machines are operated by local SIBS (known as *Multibanco*) or Euronet (typically charges hefty fees). Both are available throughout the airport.

CHARGING STATIONS Dedicated stations are not available. The few wall sockets you'll find are typically overused or defective. Bring your own powerbank.

ENTRY FORMALITIES

Valid ID United Europe or Schengen area citizens must travel with a valid identification document (Citizen Card). Valid passport and visa are required for other citizens.

Visas can be waived, depending on the visitor's country of origin.

14-day Covid-19 quarantine may be mandatory for visitors arriving from some countries; for the latest details see visitportugal.com and search for 'Covid-19'.

GETTING TO THE CITY CENTRE

Metro Red Line connects the airport to Alameda (Green Line), Saldanha (Yellow Line) and, the final stop, São Sebastião (Blue Line). The station is a few steps away from the arrivals hall, to your right. Buy tickets from automatic vending machines or ticket offices at the station.

Aerobus operates two routes: Route 1 to Cais do Sodré via Entrecampos, Campo Pequeno, Saldanha, Picoas, Marquês de Pombal, Avenida da Liberdade, Restauradores, Rossio and Praça do Comércio; Route 2 travels nonstop to Sete Rios. Purchase the 24-hour pass online at aerobus.pt or aboard the bus.

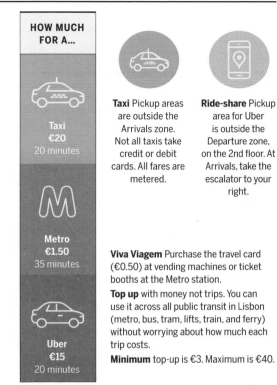

HOW MUCH FOR A...

Taxi
€20
20 minutes

Metro
€1.50
35 minutes

Uber
€15
20 minutes

Taxi Pickup areas are outside the Arrivals zone. Not all taxis take credit or debit cards. All fares are metered.

Ride-share Pickup area for Uber is outside the Departure zone, on the 2nd floor. At Arrivals, take the escalator to your right.

Viva Viagem Purchase the travel card (€0.50) at vending machines or ticket booths at the Metro station.

Top up with money not trips. You can use it across all public transit in Lisbon (metro, bus, tram, lifts, train, and ferry) without worrying about how much each trip costs.

Minimum top-up is €3. Maximum is €40.

PORTUGAL ARRIVING

OTHER POINTS OF ENTRY

Other airports you can fly into are Porto (closer for exploring the North) and Faro (best for travellers spending time in the South: the Algarve and Alentejo). The other international airports are located on the islands: Funchal (Madeira) and Ponta Delgada (São Miguel, Azores).

International cruises arrive at Lisbon Cruise Terminal near Alfama, at the heart of Lisbon's historic centre. Sometimes cruise ships dock in Alcântara or Rocha do Conde de Óbidos instead (approximately 10km from the city centre; call an Uber or take trams 15E or 18E to Cais do Sodré).

International buses operated by Rede Expressos arrive from several Spanish destinations at Lisbon (Sete Rios; connects to Metro Blue Line and suburban train), Faro and Porto (Campo 24 de Agosto).

International train connections from Spain arrive in Lisbon and Porto from Madrid (sleeper train Lusitânia Comboio Hotel and Sud Express). There's also a train connection from Vigo (Spain) to Porto (Campanhã) and Lisbon (Oriente and Santa Apolónia).

TRANSPORT TIPS TO HELP YOU GET AROUND

To cover more land and visit remote inland areas, driving is your best option. You're not dependant on restrictive public transit schedules (some areas are only served by bus twice a day, in the morning and in the evening) and you get to stop along the way to simply admire the views or follow your urge to take a detour.

CAR HIRE

Typically, car-rental companies charge rates per 24 hours, not a calendar day. Avoid extra costs choosing the same drop-off point and pickup location.
Automatic transmission cars are in short supply and typically more expensive; most cars in Portugal are manual.

AUTOMOBILE ASSOCIATIONS

ACP – Automóvel Clube de Portugal (acp.pt) – is a good resource for road maps, queries about insurance and driving rules, tolls and how much they cost, travel and accommodation tips, and all you need to know about camping in Portugal.

CAR RENTAL PER DAY

from €60

Petrol approx €1.40/litre

Diesel approx €1.20/litre

BICYCLE The number of cycle paths is increasing in Portugal, from scenic bike routes by the coast to a robust network of bike lanes in main cities. Bring your own or rent one when you arrive.

ROAD CONDITIONS Paid-toll motorways (*autoestradas*) and high-traffic secondary roads (IPs and ICs) are generally in good condition. Smaller, toll-free roads (N or EN) are usually narrow, curvy in mountainous areas, and poorly lit at night.

DRIVING ESSENTIALS

Drive on the right.

At toll booths pay with a debit card or change. If you're renting a car, ask for the Via Verde tag to use the fast lane.

Speed limit is 50km/h in urban areas; 90km/h when driving on secondary roads; 120km/h on motorways.

.05 — Blood alcohol limit is 0.5 g/l.

18 — Legal driving age is 18 years.

Train tickets If you don't mind planning your trip far ahead, CP – Comboios de Portugal (the national railway company) – cuts long-distance train tickets by up to 56% for passengers buying an Alfa Pendular or Intercidades ticket at least five days before departure, within Portugal. Tickets are available to purchase on the website (cp.pt) or via the mobile app. You must create an account and add your credit card or PayPal details.

TUK-TUKS A popular way of getting around in main cities, tuk-tuks are not to be confused with public transit. Typically, they solicit potential clients near top attractions. Prices can be high for short distances; not all drivers are skilled.

BUS & TRAIN Along the coast, most towns and cities are well-served by a reliable and comfortable network of trains and long-distance buses. Popular destinations inland are easy to reach by bus, but rail has lacked investment in recent years, meaning that most stations are permanently closed. At the time of writing, Portugal was yet to have a fast-train connection to the rest of Europe.

PLANE TAP operates regular domestic flights from Lisbon to Porto (55min) and Faro (45min). Tickets are not cheap, so unless you need to get there fast, weigh the pros and cons of going through an airport and opt for a comfortable and hassle-free train trip.

KNOW YOUR CARBON FOOTPRINT A car trip from Lisbon to Porto would emit 70kg of carbon dioxide per passenger. The same one-way trip by bus would emit 34kg of carbon dioxide per person. A train ride would emit 19kg of carbon dioxide.

There are a number of carbon calculators online. We use Resurgence at resurgence.org/resources/carbon-calculator.html.

PORTUGAL GETTING AROUND

ROAD DISTANCE CHART (KMS)

	Lisbon	Porto	Braga	Bragança	Évora	Sintra	Setúbal	Óbidos	Olhão
Porto	314								
Braga	364	55							
Bragança	486	207	217						
Évora	133	365	415	462					
Sintra	29	330	382	504	153				
Setúbal	48	349	399	521	98	69			
Óbidos	85	241	290	418	195	97	122		
Olhão	285	559	608	730	234	306	252	350	
Faro	277	551	600	722	226	298	244	342	10

DANGERS, ANNOYANCES & SAFETY

Portugal is a relatively safe country. Crime rates are low. Observe the same precautions regarding your belongings as you would back home. Pickpockets and scammers usually gather around popular attractions and try to pass off as tourists in a crowd.

SCAMS Popular scams in the larger cities include raising funds on the street for local charities that don't exist, in exchange for a fixed-fee photo. And selling 'drugs' openly during daytime, particularly in touristy, pedestrian-only streets. The only thing these fake dealers are selling is pressed bay leaves and flour.

INSURANCE
Insurance is not compulsory to travel to Portugal but it's good to have. Consider one that covers flight cancellation and medical care. Alternatively, or additionally, EU travellers can apply for the European Health Insurance Card.

CANNABIS Although Portugal decriminalised the use and possession of all drugs, regarding addiction as a disease not a crime, not everything goes. Being caught with a small amount of cannabis for personal use (up to 25 grams) is not a crime, but don't expect to see people smoking it freely on the streets.

THEFT Mind your belongings when exploring a busy place on foot and don't leave any valuables showing inside your rented car. Pickpocketing, stealing purses and vehicle break-ins are the most common occurrences. They're mostly non-violent crimes of opportunity perpetrated by several people working as a network, targeting wallets, mobile phones and other electronic devices.

Pharmacies sell prescribed and over-the-counter medication; Parapharmacies only sell over-the-counter drugs in smaller dosages. If you're in need of paracetamol or plasters, you can safely get them at either.

MICHELE RINALDI/SHUTTERSTOCK ©

FOREST FIRES
Hot, dry, windy summers and unsustainable agricultural practices are the perfect spark for 'fire season'. Travellers should check the latest IPMA reports on wildfire risk at ipma.pt/en/risco incendio/rcm.pt.

STUDIO F22 RICARDO ROCHA/ SHUTTERSTOCK ©

Solo travel With such a low crime rate, Portugal is the third safest country in the world and one of solo travellers' favourite destinations. That said, observe the same safety precautions you would back home.

QUICK TIPS TO HELP YOU MANAGE YOUR MONEY

CREDIT CARDS Visa and MasterCard are accepted at larger chain hotels, supermarkets, cafes and restaurants, and for car rentals. Small businesses prefer cash or payments with debit cards for bills over €5 (they pay a fee for each transaction, with no extra cost to you). Businesses that don't accept cards usually display a sign stating so. Diners Club and American Express cards are not as widely accepted.

CURRENCY

Euro (€)

HOW MUCH FOR A...

espresso coffee
€0.75

glass of wine
€3–5

3-course dinner for 2 **€20–30**

VAT REFUND Non-EU residents can claim a VAT (IVA in Portugal) refund for certain purchases at places boasting the Tax Free Shopping sign. Apply at the airport.

TOURIST TAX

Travellers staying in Lisbon and Porto must pay €2 per person per night, up to €14 per person (Lisbon) or maximum seven nights (Porto). Tax is automatically included in your accommodation bill.

PAYING THE BILL

Most cafes have table service. Others have a pre-payment system. At busier establishments, staff hand you a card with your registered orders to pay at the counter when you leave.

ATMS

ATMs are practically at every corner in larger cities. Smaller towns and villages might only have the ones at the local bank branches.

CURRENCY EXCHANGE

Change currency at banks or at licensed money changers (Unicâmbio) at the airport, tourist spots or shopping centres.

DISCOUNTS & SAVINGS

Most sights, activities and public transport charge a reduced fee to seniors, children under 12 and families.

City cards The Lisboa Card includes unlimited free public transport, free entry to selected museums and attractions and deals on tours. Starts at €20 (24-hour card). Similar benefits are included in the Porto.CARD. Prices start at €6. Both cards can be purchased online and must be exchanged for a physical card at the airports' tourist information booths.

TIPPING is optional and not expected.

Restaurants No service charges are added to your bill. If you want, reward good service with a 5% tip.

Taxis Round up the fare and tell the driver to keep the change.

Guides If you want to reward spectacular service, consider giving your guide an extra €5 to €10.

POSITIVE-IMPACT TRAVEL

Tips to leave a lighter footprint, support local and have a positive impact on local communities.

ON THE ROAD

Calculate your carbon footprint There are a number of online calculators. Try resurgence.org/resources/carbon-calculator.html.

Disposable, single-use plastic As of July 2021, Portugal has banned single-use plastic. Follow the lead and use reusable bags, cups and water bottles where possible.

Tap water is safe to drink in most of Portugal. When in doubt, ask a local.

When hiking or cycling stay on the marked trails and don't disturb the local wildlife.

Forest areas are susceptible to wildfires, especially in summer. Be careful with cigarette butts if you're a smoker; all it takes is a small spark to start a fire.

Public transport Strike up conversations with locals (the football is always a good topic) by using public transport. Support local taxis over Uber.

LUIS M. VIEIRA/SHUTTERSTOCK ©

GIVE BACK

Volunteer with a Portuguese-based social enterprise Check ongoing projects and locations at impactrip.com.

Sponsor a donkey Support local NGO Aepga in protecting the Mirandese donkey (pictured), an endangered species. See aepga.pt.

Support contemporary artisans Up-and-coming Portuguese artisans are adding modern twists to traditional techniques. Check portugalmanual.com for a list of artisans to support.

Experience a rural tourism stay The surge of farms-turned-hotels prevented rural areas from becoming deserted. Consider spending some time at one of those accommodations or booking a farm tour via portugalfarmexperience.com.

Donate two hours of your time Give back by collecting food that would go to waste and giving it to those who need it most. Find out how at re-food.org.

DOS & DON'TS

Do queue if you see everyone else doing it. If in doubt who's the last in line, ask.

Don't wear your bathing suit or shorts outside of the beach area.

Don't discuss politics, religion or sports without context or reassurance from the other side that they're ready to talk about it.

LEAVE A SMALL FOOTPRINT

Get to know the the bin colours Recycling bins are widely available in large cities. Green is for glass, yellow is for plastic and packages, and blue is for paper.

Practice mindful van life Park your van at official campsites. As much as it sounds romantic to wake up to a different view every day, illegal parking disturbs local human and wild life.

Plant a tree Visit zero.ong/plante-uma-arvore to make a donation to plant one or more trees that are suitable for Portugal's environment and eco-balance.

MICHELE RINALDI/SHUTTERSTOCK ©

SUPPORT LOCAL

In cities and large towns choose small businesses over large chains, both national and international.

Eat locally Buy fresh ingredients at local markets or eat at small, family-owned restaurants with traditional food. Eat a great-value soup and sandwich combo at a cafe instead of a fast-food joint.

Buy souvenirs from local artisans Ask the local *posto de turismo* for a list of shops and ateliers.

CLIMATE CHANGE & TRAVEL

It's impossible to ignore the impact we have when travelling, and the importance of making changes where we can. Lonely Planet urges all travellers to engage with their travel carbon footprint. There are many carbon calculators online that allow travellers to estimate the carbon emissions generated by their journey; try resurgence.org/resources/carbon-calculator.html. Many airlines and booking sites offer travellers the option of offsetting the impact of greenhouse gas emissions by contributing to climate-friendly initiatives around the world. We continue to offset the carbon footprint of all Lonely Planet staff travel, while recognising this is a mitigation more than a solution.

RESOURCES

zero.ong
natural.pt
quercus.pt
impactrip.com
re-food.org

PORTUGAL RESPONSIBLE TRAVEL

UNIQUE AND LOCAL WAYS TO STAY

Accommodation in Portugal has room for all tastes and budgets, from self-catered rural homes to city-centre hostels to restored castles turned into luxury hotels. And although hitting the road in a campervan seems to be the new fad, it's nothing new for families used to summers at parques de campismo.

HOW MUCH FOR A NIGHT IN

a country home
€70

a hostel dorm
€15

a guesthouse
€40

RADIOKAFKA/SHUTTERSTOCK ©

YOUTH HOSTELS & HOSTELS

While youth hostels mostly cater to students and large groups who don't mind sharing a dorm, hostels come in many shapes and sizes. You'll find a blend of dorm, private (shared or not) and family rooms. Rates vary depending on the season, but expect to pay around €15 for a dorm bed.

ALOJAMENTO LOCAL

Although often used to classify short-term rentals available on platforms like Airbnb, Alojamento Local (AL) is an umbrella term used to designate guesthouses. At this type of accommodation breakfast is usually not provided or comes at an extra cost, private bathrooms might be optional, there is no 24/7 front-desk service and in-room amenities are limited. They're often located in the city centre or near main tourist attractions.

Rates start at approximately €40 per night in high season.

STOCKPHOTOSART/SHUTTERSTOCK ©

POUSADAS DE PORTUGAL These are a network of old monasteries, convents, forts, castles and palaces transformed into luxury hotels by the Pestana Group. Despite the modern facilities, each hotel respects the history and architectural traits of the former monuments.

Prices vary according to location, but rates start at around €100 per night.

MIGUEL ALMEIDA/SHUTTERSTOCK ©

RURAL TOURISM

Whether you want to unwind, reconnect with nature or fill up your days with outdoor adventures, make your trip memorable by staying at a privately owned country house. They come in all shapes and sizes: country hotels (HR – *Hotéis Rurais*), old manors and palaces (TH – *Turismo de Habitação*), small country houses (CC – *Casas de Campo*) and farmhouses and wine estates (AG – *Agro-turismo*).

Book in advance around peak season, long weekends and national holidays. A large breakfast of local products is usually included. Other meals may be provided upon request.

Prices vary depending on the size of the room, but the cheapest accommodation starts at about €70 per night in peak season.

LOCAL CONNECTIONS

From entire villages that have been transformed into rural tourist resorts to working family farms and wine estates, opportunities for meeting and staying with locals are myriad. Although all differing in size and facilities, the emotional or family relationship with the place is central to the character of these lodgings. Expect close contact with the community, through locally sourced products and ingredients at your breakfast table and traditional arts and crafts.

BOOKING Book in advance during peak season (mid-June to mid-September, Easter and Christmas) and long weekends. Check local and national holidays that fall on a Thursday or a Tuesday – locals often take a vacation *ponte* (bridge) day on Friday or Monday.

Lonely Planet (lonelyplanet.com/portugal/hotels) Find independent reviews, as well as recommendations on the best places to stay – and then book them online.

Aldeias de Portugal (aldeiasdeportugal.pt) A website listing most of the village tourist resorts in the country.

Solares de Portugal (solaresdeportugal.pt) Book a stay at a restored family manor, estate or country house.

Pousadas de Portugal (pousadas.pt) Official booking site for Grupo Pestana's monument and historic hotels.

Pousadas de Juventude (pousadasjuventude.pt) Official booking site for youth hostels.

Roteiro Campista (roteiro-campista.pt) Lists all the campsites in Portugal, including where to legally park campervans.

Termas de Portugal (termasdeportugal.pt) List of natural spas in Portugal. Some include accommodation and not all are open all year round.

CAMPING SITES

Camping options range from simple sites with modest facilities to large complexes of permanent campervans, often by a beach and crowded in the summer. Prices start at around €10 per person and per tent or campervan.

PORTUGAL ESSENTIALS

ESSENTIAL NUTS-AND-BOLTS

NAVIGATION
Rely on GPS to avoid getting lost on backroads when road-tripping in Portugal. On foot, don't take suggestions for granted and observe your surroundings.

SMOKING
Smoking, including e-cigarettes, is not allowed in public spaces, except within designated areas. Most restaurants and cafes don't have a smoking section.

EMERGENCIES
Call 112.
For non-urgent situations, call SNS24 (808 24 24 24; press 9 for English).

FAST FACTS

Time Zone
GMT/UTC

Country Code
351

Electricity
230V/50Hz

GOOD TO KNOW

If there's a queue, respect it and apologise if you unintentionally cut in line.

If you're carrying large luggage, opt for a ride-share or taxi instead of public transport.

The legal drinking age in Portugal is 18 and it's legal to drink in public.

EU and Schengen area citizens don't need a visa, just a valid ID.

Citizens of 60+ countries can travel to Portugal without a visa. (vistos.mne.gov.pt)

ACCESSIBLE TRAVEL

Larger chain hotels will have wheelchair-friendly rooms; check before booking at smaller accommodations.

Main train and metro stations have lifts, though they're few or poorly located.

Cities' historic centres aren't wheelchair- or visually-impaired-friendly. Slippery, poorly maintained cobblestones and narrow streets make it difficult to navigate.

Braille descriptions are available at most museums and public services.

Accessible beach award honours beaches and other swimming areas for their wheelchair-friendly facilities. As of now, more than 200 places are certified.

tur4all.pt is a global, official resource for accessible travel in Portugal. You can also download the app for iOS and Android.

PUBLIC HOLIDAYS

There are 13 public holidays in Portugal. Some businesses and non-essential services may be closed.

BORDER CROSSING

Foreign nationals arriving in Portugal from Spain must submit a Declaration of Entry within three days of arrival.

PUBLIC TOILETS

In major cities, public toilets are scarce. Shopping centres, markets and cafes (customers only) are your best bet.

FAMILY TRAVEL

Reduced fares for public transport, museums and attractions are available for children under 10 or 12.

Traditional trams are too narrow for strollers.

Kids menus are more frequent at chain restaurants. At more traditional spots, ask if they can make something not on the menu, order a *meia dose* (half portion) or bring your own food.

High chairs are available at most restaurants.

Child seats aren't available in taxis. If hiring a car, request one in advance.

VACCINATIONS

Not mandatory for visiting Portugal, unless you're travelling from a Yellow Fever Zone. At the time of writing, Covid-19 vaccination wasn't compulsory to enter the country, but a negative PCR test was. Check updates at covid19estamoson.gov.pt.

CLEAN & SAFE SEAL

Turismo de Portugal created this seal to highlight businesses and activities compliant with hygiene and safety measures regarding prevention and control of Covid-19. The programme covers training and compliance inspections. Look for the logo before booking tours and hotels or consult the list at portugalcleanandsafe.com.

LGBTIQ+ TRAVELLERS

Outright discrimination is unusual (or unreported), but outside major urban and touristic areas (Lisbon, Porto, Algarve) same-sex couples are still seen as outside the norm.

Lisbon has the largest gay scene. Gay communities are more discreet elsewhere.

Same-sex marriage has been legal in Portugal since 2010.

Law of Gender Identity, passed in 2011, allows transgender persons to legally change their gender on official documents.

ILGA is an NGO assisting the LGBTIQ+ community. Check ilga-portugal.pt for updated reports and support groups.

LANGUAGE

Portuguese pronunciation is not difficult because most sounds are also found in English. The exceptions are the nasal vowels (represented in our pronunciation guides by ng after the vowel), which are pronounced as if you're trying to make the sound through your nose; and the strongly rolled r (represented by rr in our pronunciation guides). Also note that the symbol zh sounds like the 's' in 'pleasure'. In our pronunciation guides stressed syllables are indicated with italics.
To enhance your trip with a phrasebook, visit shop.lonely planet.com.

BASICS

Hello.	*Olá.*	o·*laa*
Goodbye.	*Adeus.*	a·de·*oosh*
Yes.	*Sim.*	seeng
No.	*Não.*	nowng
Please.	*Por favor.*	poor fa·*vor*
Thank you.	*Obrigado.*	o·bree·*gaa*·doo (m)
		o·bree·*gaa*·da (f)
You're welcome.	*De nada.*	de *naa*·da
Excuse me.	*Faz favor.*	faash fa·*vor*
Sorry.	*Desculpe.*	desh·*kool*·pe

What's your name?
Qual é o seu nome?   kwaal e oo se·oo *no*·me

My name is ...
O meu nome é ...   oo *me*·oo *no*·me e ...

Do you speak English?
Fala inglês?   faa·la eeng·*glesh*

I don't understand.
Não entendo.   nowng eng·*teng*·doo

TIME & NUMBERS

What time is it?	*Que horas são?*	kee o·rash sowng
It's (10) o'clock.	*São (dez) horas.*	sowng (desh) o·rash
Half past (10).	*(Dez) e meia.*	(desh) e *may*·a

morning	*manhã*	ma·*nyang*
afternoon	*tarde*	*taar*·de
evening	*noite*	*noy*·te
yesterday	*ontem*	*ong*·teng
today	*hoje*	o·zhe
tomorrow	*amanhã*	aa·ma·*nyang*

1	*um*	oong	**6**	*seis*	saysh
2	*dois*	doysh	**7**	*sete*	se·te
3	*três*	tresh	**8**	*oito*	oy·too
4	*quatro*	kwaa·troo	**9**	*nove*	no·ve
5	*cinco*	seeng·koo	**10**	*dez*	desh

EMERGENCIES

Help!	*Socorro!*	soo·*ko*·rroo
Go away!	*Vá-se embora!*	vaa·se eng·*bo*·ra
I'm ill.	*Estou doente.*	shtoh doo·*eng*·te
Call ...!	*Chame ...!*	*shaa*·me ...
a doctor	*um médico*	oong *me*·dee·koo
the police	*a polícia*	a poo·*lee*·sya

Index

250

PORTUGAL INDEX B-C

000 Map pages